FIXING THE U.S. CRIMINAL JUSTICE SYSTEM

Paul Brakke

Author of
The Price of Justice in America,
Cops Aren't Such Bad Guys,
The Great National Divides,
and
American Justice?

TABLE OF CONTENTS

ACKNOWLEDGMENTS

I am indebted to Gini Graham Scott for much help in the preparation of this book. She assisted with editing, some additional insights, and formatting the book for publication.

Further, I would like to acknowledge the assistance of publicist Jana Collins.

Finally, since I have no first-hand knowledge of prison, I have obtained valuable insights on life in prison for the first two chapters from four individuals who have either spent time in prison or have or have had family members there. All have asked to remain anonymous, but I wish to express my appreciation to them.

INTRODUCTION

My own odyssey into the criminal justice system began in 2008, when my wife was falsely accused of trying to run over a 12-year old boy in our neighborhood. What happened next was frightening and revealed to us many flaws in the criminal justice system. I won't go into what happened to us here. If you're interested, read my book *American Justice?*, where I detail our ordeal.

Since then, I became more and more interested in the criminal justice system. As I read more, it became clear to me that what happened to us as normal conservative law-abiding citizens could happen to anyone. Moreover, what happened to us was nothing compared to what happens to thousands of victims of the system each and every day. Because many of these problems have not been written up by conservatives, I've had to read and even refer to some material from liberal sources, but I've made sure that any claims I make are free from liberal bias.

This book represents an analysis of the problems encountered by victims of this system and the contributions made to it by police, prosecutors, judges and the media. I hope to showcase some of the glaring problems in the criminal justice system in order to motivate enough people and government officials to seek change. Many books of this genre provide copious criticisms of the system but little in the way of detailed constructive suggestions. In this book, each chapter concludes with a set of Suggested Solutions.

I apologize to those African-American readers who may feel offended by my frequent use of the term "blacks." I do this only because I grew up in a time before the term "African-Americans" was in common usage, but the term "blacks" was.

CHAPTER 1: OUR CRIMINAL JUSTICE SYSTEM IS A NATIONAL SHAME

One out of every 32 Americans — approximately 7.2 million adults as of this writing — is on probation, on parole, or in prison at any given time. In what has been described by liberals as the prison-industrial complex, approximately 2.3 million Americans are in prison, nearly one in one hundred adults.[1] African Americans like Barack Obama and Michelle Alexander are fond of pointing out that we have 5% of the world's population, yet 25% of the world's prisoners.[2]

Our country has the highest rate of incarceration in the world — higher than Russia, China, or Iran. It is eight times higher than the rate in Germany. And it's eight times higher than we had ourselves thirty years ago.[3] We'll never be able to "Make America Great Again" if we don't fix this problem.

Who realized this was happening? Very few of us. This high rate of incarceration was all news to me. To most of us, prisons are invisible. As Eugene Jarecki pointed out on a 2012 Charlie Rose program, the public is largely unaware of the prison situation, because prisons are located in rural areas and the prison population is relatively powerless.[4]

It's enormously expensive to incarcerate so many people. The costs of incarceration, parole, and probation in the corrections "industry" amount to over $70 billion

---

[1]Steven Nolan, "The Prison Industrial Complex", *The Intelhub.com*; http://theintelhub.com/2012/05/17prison-industrial-complex

[2]Robert A. Ferguson, *Inferno: An Anatomy of American Punishment*, Harvard University Press, 2014.

[3] Michelle Alexander, *The New Jim Crow: Mass Incarceration in the Age of Colorblindness*, The New Press, 2012.

[4] Charlie Rose; http://www.tv.com/shows/charlie-rose/watch/marion-cotillard-andrew-solomon-a-discussion-about-prison-reform-2615132

annually.[5] This amount is as much as the food stamp program.[6] This clearly is an expensive proposition the U.S. can't afford, given a debt in the trillions and a need to raise the debt ceiling, or the U.S. will go broke and default on its debts, creating a world-wide crisis. State governments are strapped and increasingly concerned with the costs of incarcerating so many. The Republican governor of my state Arkansas opted not to build a new prison and instead is sending inmates to a neighboring state, saving approximately $70 million in the process.

How did we get to this point?

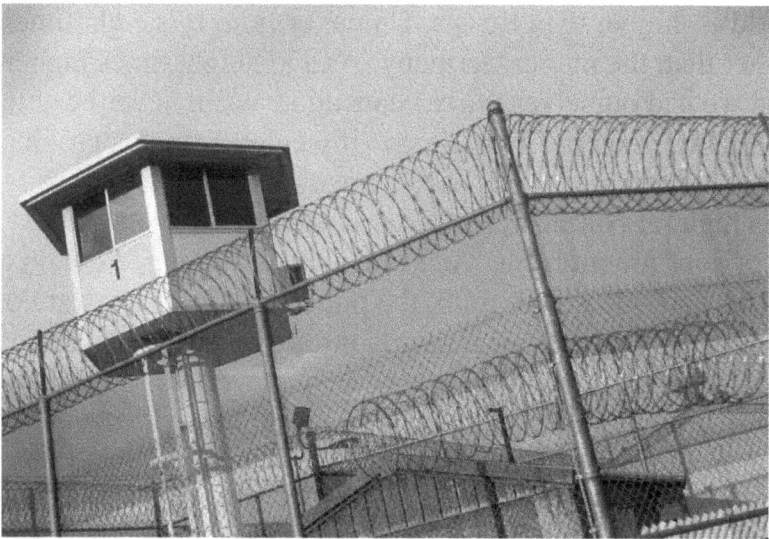

---

[5] David Wolman, "The New Economics of Crime and Punishment", http://www.wired.com/2012/11/st_essay_convictonomics

[6] Ed Morrisey, "Sessions: Food Stamps Programs Expanding in Costs, Size," *Hot Air*; http://hotair.com/archives/2012/06/27/sessions-food-stamp-programs-exploding-in-costs-size

The Deleterious Effects of the War on Drugs

As Eugene Jarecki pointed out on the aforementioned Charlie Rose program, even employees in the criminal justice system, such as cops, judges, and prison guards, recognize that the drug war is not being won. The drug war is taking money from budgets that could be better spent elsewhere. There are perverse incentives in the system to keep this costly war going. For example, the officer who makes drug arrests gets overtime for doing the paperwork for each arrest. As a result, he can make many more arrests than an investigator who spends more time solving a homicide case. Thus, the cop who pursues the drug arrests is the one who gets promoted.[4]

Mass incarceration has truly blighted our inner cities. In addition, there are political consequences. Rural counties where prisons are located gain more representation by having a larger population in each census. However, liberals complain that prisoners cannot vote, and their presence instead strengthens the voting power of the local population, which is predominantly white. These prisoners are removed from the areas where they used to live — usually the inner cities, which reduces the voting power of those areas. But as evidenced from numerous news stories, liberals tend to object to voter ID laws intended to reduce voter fraud, as well.

The growth of the prison industry is reflected in prison trade shows and in the pressure on local representatives in state government as well as Congress to support prisons to bring business to a particular region.[4] Many people, especially those who are politically liberal, do not feel we should regard the incarceration of prisoners as a business and feel it should not be tainted by business concerns. However, incarceration is very expensive. In 2010, it cost between

$14,603 and $60,076 per year, depending on the state,[7] and therefore these expenses do need to be managed with as little waste as possible. Oftentimes state and federal governments are poor stewards of taxpayer dollars, yet business interests can profit from the system at the expense of prisoners and their families, whether the prisons are private, state run or federal.

Prisoners require a degree of compassion and adequate medical care while in custody, as well as opportunities for rehabilitation through education and support groups. Injured or ill prisoners incur higher costs, and there is a PR nightmare when prisoners become seriously ill or die, worse still if prison riots and rebellions to protest bad treatment occur. Investment in rehabilitation and jobs training contributes to ex-prisoners being more able to find jobs after their release in prison, and they are less likely to offend again, resulting in lower recidivism rates. Not only are employed ex-prisoners less likely to engage in criminal activity because they have jobs, but they can contribute to the economy, too. And families with an ex-convict who has a job are more likely to remain intact, which strengthens the economy and family values, as well.

By the same token, reforming the government's drug policies could have positive economic benefits, too, since many of those imprisoned were arrested for drug offenses. Yet the war on drugs has failed to stop drug use or the spread of international gangs. Instead, the underground nature of the drug industry has led to a large criminal element involved in producing, distributing, and selling drugs. In turn, that has not only drawn gangs in the U.S., Mexico, and other countries into providing illegal drugs for U.S. customers, but it has resulted in increased costs for law enforcement, the courts,

---

[7] https://static.prisonpolicy.org/scans/vera/the-price-of-prisons.pdf

and corrections, in processing drug dealers and users through the system.

As former Senator Jim Webb has pointed out, "A dangerous form of organized and sometimes deadly gang activity has infiltrated America's towns and cities. It comes largely from our country's southern border, and much of the criminal activity centers around the movement of illegal drugs."[8] Much of this criminal activity comes from Mexican drug cartels, as they engage in extremely brutal actions to spread their profitable business enterprises through our cities.

Thus, one approach has traditionally been to try to curtail the import and sale of these drugs, an approach advocated by the Trump administration in securing our southern border. Yet, as long as there has been high demand, the drug sellers have found multiple channels for bringing drugs to the end-user customer, which has meant the prohibition approach has not been effective, while costing astronomical amounts of money.

Educating kids and adults against using drugs has not fixed the problem either, given peer pressure and how good the drugs make the users feel at first. Before they realize it, they become addicted.

The medical profession has contributed to this problem by overprescribing opiates for pain. At present we have a clear opioid addiction epidemic that everyone agrees has reached crisis proportions, both in rural as well as urban areas. Many more treatment centers must be opened to treat these addicts rather than merely incarcerating them.

On the other hand, the American public is growing ever more in favor of a permissive attitude toward marijuana. Marijuana may well be less harmful than alcohol, and our

---

[8]James Webb, "What's Wrong with Our Prisons?" *Parade,* March 29, 2009, p. 5.

prison and jail costs could go down considerably if marijuana possession were decriminalized to a level similar to a speeding ticket. Some states have even voted in favor of legalization and taxation, particularly since traditional approaches have proved very costly and aren't working. Marijuana represents an unusual issue where states' rights advocates are now advocating permissiveness, while the federal government is resisting. In addition, younger adults without children are generally in favor of less restriction of marijuana use, while parents of children have legitimate concerns. Medical marijuana appears to represent a first step in the direction of approval of recreational marijuana in many states. If the federal government fails to clamp down on marijuana use, the experience of those states which have approved its use should be carefully monitored, particularly for its effects on marijuana use by under-age adolescents, whose brain development might be adversely affected.

Disproportionate Effects on Minority Communities

Another good reason to curtail the costly war on drugs is that a serious side effect of this war has been the unintended societal effects on minority communities. While the majority of illegal drug users and dealers throughout the U.S. are white, three-fourths of all the people incarcerated for drug offenses are African-Americans and Latinos. In 2006, one in nine 20-35 year old black men was behind bars, and far more were on probation or parole. In 2000, eight times as many whites were imprisoned for drug offenses as in 1983 (a huge increase); yet 22 times as many Latinos and 26 times as many African-Americans were imprisoned as in 1983.[3]

In some states, it's even worse:

❖ In 2000... in seven states, African-Americans constituted 80-90% of all drug offenders sent to prison.

❖ In at least 15 states, blacks are admitted to prison on drug charges at a rate 20 to 57 times greater than that of white men.[3]

The consequences of these high arrest and conviction rates are that African-American males are seven times more likely to be incarcerated than white males. As a result, one out of fifteen African-American men are in prison, compared to one out of thirty-six Hispanic men and one out of 106 white men. Shockingly, one in three black men will spend some time in prison during the course of their lifetime.[9] That wrecks the black family structure, since it leaves the family without a provider and with young black males lacking a good male role model to help them grow up to become good citizens. This high incarceration rate for African-American males thus perpetuates crime in the black community.

---

[9] "1 in 3 Black Men Go To Prison? The 10 Most Disturbing Facts about Racial Inequality in the U.S. Criminal Justice System." *AlterNet*, March 17, 2012.

The racial disparity in imprisonment results in the fact that almost half (49.4%) of incarcerated parents are black, so that African-American children are 7.5 times more likely and Hispanic children 2.5 times more likely than white children to have a parent in prison.[10] An article in the liberal *New Yorker* magazine even reported that, "In truth, there are more black men in the grip of the criminal-justice system — in prison, on probation, or on parole — than were in slavery."[11] In turn, the effects on the economy are astronomical, given the costs involved in housing, feeding, and otherwise caring for them in prison, given the costs of imprisoning one inmate at over $30,000 a year, depending on the state.[12] And these costs are not only borne by the state or federal budget but are further vastly inflated by losses in economic productivity and family upheaval. In many instances, the incarcerated individual could instead be given a shorter sentence, released into some kind of community-based program, or required to pay restitution rather than being jailed at all.

Black civil rights advocate Michelle Alexander contends this high incarceration rate for blacks happens in three phases:

1. Police apprehend more inner city blacks on drug charges, because that is easier and more lucrative than arrests for other crimes, and the police often employ racial profiling.

2. After their arrest, minority defendants generally do not receive legal representation due to their low-income status. Then, whether guilty or not, they are

---

[10] "Families with Incarcerated Parents Fact Sheet."

[11] "The Caging of America: Why Do We Lock So Many People Up," *The New Yorker*, January 30, 2012;
http://www.newyorker.com/arts/critics/atlarge/2012/01/30/120130crat_atlarge_gopnik

[12] https://static.prisonpolicy.org/scans/vera/the-price-of-prisons.pdf

pressured to plead guilty and face harsh drug sentencing guidelines.

3. The laws that affect ex-cons' lives are debilitating, since they deny employment, housing, education, and public benefits. Unable to surmount these obstacles, most ex-cons never reintegrate back into society and eventually return to prison. The recidivism rate for minority ex-convicts is 70%.[3]

So again, it is important to consider the high costs of both processing at all stages of contact with the criminal justice system and the loss of productive employment to society.

Once branded as felons, ex-cons face legal discrimination for the rest of their lives, resulting in high costs to society as a whole. They are barred from getting food stamps and obtaining public housing for themselves and their families. Whenever they apply for a job, at most companies they have to check a box to indicate they have been in prison. They are behind the proverbial eight ball for the rest of their lives; no wonder so many fail to re-integrate into society and wind up back in prison.

Our prison policy discourages stable relationships like marriage, which is particularly fragile in the African-American community. With many of the families of prisoners now living below the poverty line, U.S. welfare policy contributes to the problem by providing inadequate assistance to intact families. The AFDC (Aid to Families with Dependent Children) program unintentionally encourages African-American males to stay away from the home, too. All the way back in 1965, liberal Senator Daniel Patrick Moynihan identified the deleterious effects of this program, stating, "The steady expansion of this welfare program, as of public assistance programs in general, can be taken as a measure of the steady disintegration of the [African-American] family structure."[13] Then, this disintegration of black families can be translated into economic costs and losses to society, too, and the long-term effects on other family members result in even more negative economic consequences,

As an example of these negative consequences, both economic and social, the children of prisoners and ex-cons are increasingly troubled, and more likely to suffer from mental illness. They are likely to be poor, homeless, academically-challenged, and physically aggressive. Often they end up in prison themselves, continuing the vicious cycle.[14] Impoverished urban black ghettos that are cauldrons for crime are both the cause and the consequence.

Something, obviously, is awry in America — one of the most "developed" countries in the world! Why do we have such a high rate of incarceration in our nation? What are the staggering costs to society?[15] And what can we do about it?

---

[13] Office of Policy Planning and Research, United States Department of Labor, "The Negro Family: The Case for National Action", March 1965; http://www.intellectualtakeout.org/content/quotes-welfare-state-family

[14] Erik Eckholm, "With Higher Numbers of Prisoners Comes a Tide of Troubled Children," *New York Times,* July 5, 2009.

[15] Some financial estimates run over a trillion dollars (Carrie Pettus-Davis, Washington Univ. St. Louis, referred to by Matt Ferner,*The Full Cost Of Incarceration In The U.S. Is Over $1 Trillion, Study Finds* ;http://www.huffingtonpost.com/entry/mass-incarceration-cost_us_57d82d99e4b09d7a687fde21), and that's only the financial part.

Suggested Solutions

Serious reform is needed in the prisons. This certainly won't be an easy fix, but there are ways that it is possible to reduce both the devastation for individuals and families and the economic costs to society. How can we fix the system?

➤ Abolish mandatory minimum sentencing in cases of nonviolent drug cases. This could reduce the prison population by several hundred thousand. While Attorney General Jeff Sessions does not appear to be in favor, mandatory minimum sentencing is primarily a state and local issue, not a federal one, since most prisoners are in state facilities.

➤ Set up more re-entry centers to house prisoners in their last six months of incarceration. These re-entry centers can reduce the staggeringly high recidivism rate, whereby two thirds of those released wind up re-arrested within three years.[16] These centers can train prisoners in life skills, handling finances, and job procurement at only about half the cost of a state's prison.[17] Many states have already set up such centers.

➤ Reduce the vast number of security guards but increase the number of counselors in mandated drug treatment facilities for convicts and newly released ex-cons. Such a change might go a long way towards lowering the high recidivism rate for felons, and thus ultimately

---

[16] Bureau of Justice statistics, 2005.
[17] Roy Ockert, "Study offers suggestions to keep prison inmates from returning," The Pine Bluff Commercial, December 19, 2014, http://pbcommercial.com/columns-blogs/roy-ockert/study-offers-suggestions-keep-prison-inmates-returning

reduce violence on our streets and the high prison population. Again, less violence and a smaller prison population mean less financial drain on society.

➢ By reducing the enormous costs of incarcerating prisoners who do not require imprisonment, funds can be released for many other worthwhile programs at the federal and state level. This can include federal and state courts, both currently in serious financial difficulty and unable to provide speedy trials.[18,19]

➢ Correspondingly, reduce our over 95% reliance on the plea bargain system, which penalizes those who cannot afford to hire a lawyer or to bail themselves out of jail while awaiting trial.

❖ Further details are in my book THE COSTLY U.S. PRISON SYSTEM: TOO COSTLY IN DOLLARS, NATIONAL PRESTIGE AND LIVES.

---

[18]"Federal Court Programs Threatened by Budget Cuts, Official Warns Congress," *The BLT*, *Blog of Legal Times: Law and Lobbying in the Nation's Capital*, March 28, 2012, http://legaltimes.typepad.com/blt/2012/03/federal-courts-programs-threatened-by-budget-cuts-official-warns-congress.html
[19] Andrew Cohen, "At State Courts, Budgets Are Tight and Lives are In Limbo", *The Atlantic*, September 23, 2011, http://www.theatlantic.com/national/archive/2011/09/at-state-courts-budgets-are-tight-and-lives-are-in-limbo/245558/#

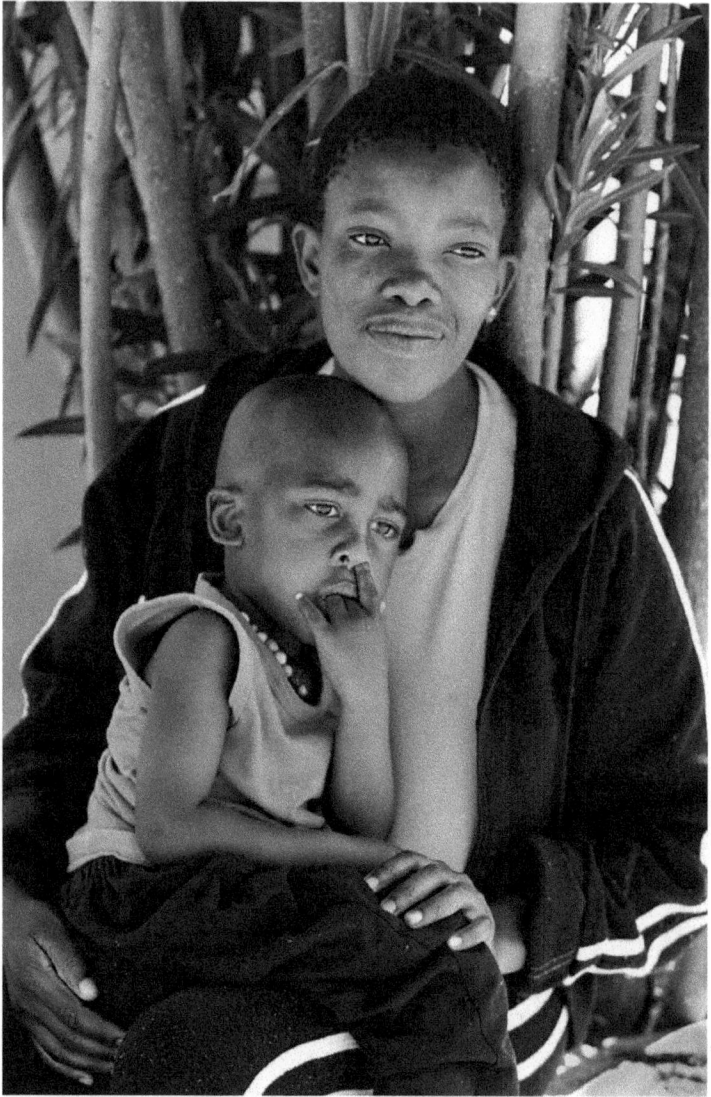

CHAPTER 2: FAMILIES SUFFER SEVERE COLLATERAL DAMAGE

Generally, the term collateral damage refers to unintended damage after a military operation, which can include the destruction of buildings and properties not related to mission objectives. Collateral damage may also be applied to any case that goes through the criminal justice system, as the process impacts entire family units — spouses, children, parents, and relatives — and all of the defendant's relationships. Such unintended consequences occur at all stages of a prosecution, from the initial charge, to the trial and verdict. If the charged person is found guilty, these consequences continue during that person's probation or imprisonment.

But even if the result is a not-guilty verdict, there still is collateral damage. For instance, once a person is charged with a crime, everyone related to that individual can experience a huge financial, emotional, mental, and physical toll. Whether or not a defendant actually goes to prison, the damages to the lifestyle and the career of a partner or family member can be considerable. And as the potential for the defendant's long sentence mounts, the feeling of unfairness by family members can lead to significant anger and hurt — emotions that do not simply disappear when a charged individual is found innocent. Regrettably, these everyday side effects of our judicial system have largely been ignored.

As Americans, we respect family values. Yet when it comes to the criminal justice system, we oftentimes permit family values to be trampled. And this collateral damage is not only to the bonds in the family, but there is economic fallout to taxpayers, too, from costs of incarceration, loss of income, and the negative effects of broken families.

The Impact on Families

A Loss of Privacy

When a case goes to trial or otherwise gets media attention, everyone in a family is affected. Friends and neighbors often respond differently than before or turn a cold shoulder. Children get teased or taunted at school. Relatives may get suspicious. Strangers get nosy. In short, life is no longer the same.

Jon Benet Ramsey's parents were subjected to a witch-hunt and media frenzy for many years, all because of the suspicions that John Ramsey had killed his six-year-old daughter, a beauty pageant queen. Suspicion fell on Patsy as the killer, too. Eventually, to gain some sort of privacy and escape the media's unrelenting glare, John and his wife Patsy sold their home in Colorado and moved out of state. Yet even there, the media, intent on keeping the national story alive, haunted the couple. It was not until 2008 — after Patsy Ramsey's death from cancer — that John Ramsey was no longer considered a suspect. Questions were raised about missed clues on the scene that suggested the entry of a killer into the house, possibly through a basement window. At that time, the Boulder District Attorney formally apologized to John and his family for the "cloud of suspicion" they had to endure for over a decade.[20] We'll revisit this case in Chapter 6.

---

[20] http://www.people.com/people/archive/article/0,,20580704,00.html

Psychological Damage/Familial Fall-Out

Several aspects of a criminal case can produce long-term negative psychological damage for the entire family. For children, the process of taking an accused parent away can be particularly unsettling. And if the police come to the family home to make an arrest or further investigate after arresting a family member, they may tear apart the residence looking for potential evidence to add to their case. The police are initially limited to searching only the areas of the house under the control of the individual they have arrested. However, they can search further if their initial search leads them to notice other evidence of criminal behavior, such as if they see drug paraphernalia in an adjacent room. Ultimately, they may find a reason to search the whole house. If this occurs, family members and/or others can only look on helplessly, unable to halt the process. Chances are, bedrooms are invaded or journals and computers are reviewed and sometimes taken for evidence.

Family members can feel unnerved if they get a call from the accused, who has typically placed this first call from jail to say he or she has been arrested. During that conversation, the accused may ask them to quickly get bail together to "Get me of jail." But if the family doesn't have immediate access to the full amount requested, they may have to pay a bail bondsman 10% of the total. If the required financial resources are not available, then family members must meet with the accused in jail, where they, too, may often feel subjected to degradation and humiliation, such as from the careful search they are subjected to before being let in to see the incarcerated prisoner.

If the accused manages to return home, family members can still feel unnerved and vulnerable by what has happened. Unhappily, this is only the beginning. Family members will be called upon to do even more to contribute more time and money as the legal process continues. For instance, they generally are asked to appear at a series of hearings, as well as find and meet with a lawyer to help their loved one.

Far worse still is the collateral damage experienced by families of those in prison. One source of fall-out for families and children is the feelings of shame and social stigma that comes from having a family member in prison. Many family members don't tell even their closest friends if a family member is incarcerated in order to maintain this family "secret." As a result, they miss out on any support their friends might provide, and virtually no other support in the form of counseling or financial assistance is available for the families of individuals processed through the criminal justice system. As author Creasie Finney Hairston points out, this fallout for families has long been largely ignored:

> "The well-being of prisoners' families and children has not been an important part of this social policy agenda... services and activities that assist prisoners in carrying out family roles and responsibilities have seldom been included in the strategic plans of social service agencies or corrections departments."[21]

Moreover, visiting the person imprisoned can be traumatic, discouraging families from wanting to visit again. As Hairston further notes:

> "For many families and friends of prisoners, the visit to a prison is a lesson in humility,

---

[21] Creasie Finney Hairston "Prisoners and Families: Parenting Issues During Incarceration", Jane Addams College of Social Work, University of Illinois at Chicago, December 2001, http://aspe.hhs.gov/hsp/prison2home02/hairston.htm

intimidation and frustration and a highly charged and anxiety producing event. It is not unusual for visitors, the majority of whom are women and children, to endure many indignities.... long waits sometimes in facilities without seating, toilets, and water; the lack of nutritious food in visiting room vending machines and the absence of activities for children. Body frisks and intrusive searches, rude treatment by staff, and hot, dirty and crowded visiting rooms are the norm in many prisons. Visitors may be denied entry to the prison for diverse reasons, including constantly changing dress codes, no identification for children, and ion drug scanners that inaccurately signal that a visitor is carrying drugs."[22]

Some incarcerated parents prefer that their children not visit them in prison or make any effort to contact them, commonly because they are embarrassed or ashamed and feel the visit will hurt their child more. They may ask other family members to keep their imprisonment secret in order to "protect" their child.

At the same time, many corrections and social services professionals discourage prison visits by children, because they are concerned about the effect of the oppressive prison environment on them and legitimately concerned such children may come to accept incarceration as "normal."[22]

---

[22] Creasie Finney Hairston "Prisoners and Families: Parenting Issues During Incarceration", Jane Addams College of Social Work, University of Illinois at Chicago, December 2001, http://aspe.hhs.gov/hsp/prison2home02/hairston.htm

Deterioration of Family Units

Many state laws allow for the termination of parental rights solely on the basis of criminal activity[23] — which means those states can place any children in state custody and effectively break up the family. Alternatively, parental rights can be terminated if "parents fail to communicate regularly with their children."[24]

Marital or romantic relationships can suffer significant, sometimes insurmountable, damage due to the separation when someone is imprisoned. The resulting physical and emotional separation from loved ones contributes to divorces, breakups for unmarried couples, disruptions in parenting, and child custody battles that devastate both parents and children. As Hairston notes:

> "Couples are usually denied sexual intimacy and are unable to engage in the day-to-day interactions, experiences and sharing which sustain marital and other intimate, adult relationships. Loneliness and missing each other and a host of other feelings about the separation, justice system, criminal activity, and each partner's honesty and faithfulness are common."[24]

---

[23] Philip Genty "Incarcerated Parents and the Adoption and Safe Families Act ("ASFA"): A Challenge for Correctional Service Providers," *ICCA Journal on Community Corrections*, November 2001, 42-47.

[24] Creasie Finney Hairston "Prisoners and Families: Parenting Issues During Incarceration", Jane Addams College of Social Work, University of Illinois at Chicago, December 2001, http://aspe.hhs.gov/hsp/prison2home02/hairston.htm

Financial Woes

Another huge problem that soon may arise is financial, including, according to Hairston:

> "...the costs of maintaining the household, the loss of income of the imprisoned parent who was contributing to the household, legal fees associated with criminal defense and appeals, the costs associated with maintaining contact during imprisonment and the costs of maintaining the prisoner while he (or she) is in prison."[25]

Maintaining contact with the person in prison can be expensive, since prison visits are very costly due to the family's need for transportation (often to a remote location), meals, vending machine snacks, and perhaps the cost of a hotel or motel for those visiting overnight. The family too must pay for something as necessary and commonplace as the prisoner's phone calls. Unable to own cell phones in prison and denied Internet access, prisoners can only call collect, and this can rack up big bills. Low-income families normally cannot afford these costs, especially if the prisoner was the primary source of financial support for the family.

Family members of incarcerated prisoners may additionally need to take on roles previously played by the incarcerated family member. They may have to pitch in and help out, or take on full or major responsibility for something the incarcerated family member used to routinely handle, such as being the primary breadwinner. Grandmothers, sisters, and aunts might take on the childrearing

---

[25] Creasie Finney Hairston "Prisoners and Families: Parenting Issues During Incarceration", Jane Addams College of Social Work, University of Illinois at Chicago, December 2001, http://aspe.hhs.gov/hsp/prison2home02/hairston.htm

responsibilities of a prisoner's young children; spouses may need to take on extra work to support the family.[26]

Those relatives who take care of the children of mothers or fathers in prison undergo additional financial expenses, as it falls to them to supply the children with food, clothing, any necessary daycare, and/or transportation arrangements to get the kids to school.[26]

Other expenses that families of incarcerated individuals must bear include the costs to provide prisoners with everyday items not provided by the prison. These include toiletries, reading materials, stamps, food, and clothing. The prisoners also pay indirectly for other services, such as when the prison places a levy on the funds in their account, which have been deposited for any paid work they do. Such a levy may include charges for medical visits, health care, institutional fines, and child support.[27]

Besides the direct costs to the prisoner's family, there are costs to both state and federal coffers due to the cost of both social services and financial assistance. One such cost occurs because without the prisoner's financial contribution, some families seek outside assistance, such as Medicaid, relative foster care payments, or public assistance welfare benefits. Ironically, these costs may be lessened because some families will choose not to seek this outside assistance even if they need it. This may occur if the request could expose the family to "external scrutiny," which can risk an official action (such as the authorities removing the children from the homes of the relatives and friends who are caring for them and placing the kids in foster care).

---

[26] Creasie Finney Hairston "Prisoners and Families: Parenting Issues During Incarceration", Jane Addams College of Social Work, University of Illinois at Chicago, December 2001, http://aspe.hhs.gov/hsp/prison2home02/hairston.htm
[27] Ibid.

The consequences of lockups therefore are horrendous for prisoners' families, and all too often families become incentivized to break up, due to the high cost of maintaining contact and supporting a prisoner in prison. Thus, incarceration erodes family values, while often resulting in high costs to the taxpayer for some families that obtain assistance from government programs.

A Family's Future Picture, Financial and Otherwise

According to some studies, many inmates often start to withdraw from being actively involved in their children's lives, if they discover their former partner has started a new relationship. At the same time, mothers whose partners are in prison often choose new boyfriends who are abusive, something that ultimately can cost them custody of their own children. Besides suffering from the decline in family income from a parent in prison, mothers and their children can face further economic difficulties. Often the families of incarcerated fathers cut off any financial assistance to the mother if the mother has given up on the father as a partner. This cut-off of funds can then lead mothers to depression and criminal activities like prostitution, some things that further traumatize the children.[28] In addition, there can be social and economic costs when family members get involved in such criminal activity to support themselves. This collateral damage becomes worse still when family members become ensnared in the criminal justice system themselves, if caught engaging in illegal acts like prostitution or theft.

---

[28] Jeremy Travis and Michelle Waul, "Prisoners Once Removed: The Impact of Incarceration on Children, Families, and Communities", Urban Institute, 2004.

Another indirect, but very real, form of collateral damage for families is the loss of income that occurs when a defendant who has a professional or business license is no longer able to practice in that profession or run that business, even after release. Often defendants plead guilty to a lesser felony, not realizing it could jeopardize their chances of future employment.

Often, too, convicted defendants lose their licenses or find it difficult to secure employment after they have paid their dues, despite laws that encourage employers not to discriminate against previously convicted employees.

Moreover, there are other wide ranging prohibitions and disqualifications that ex-offenders commonly face after completing their criminal sentences. For example, in Arizona, ex-cons are blocked from public and housing benefits and face restrictions on employment and voting. The irony is that these additional consequences generally last longer than the direct sentence, so these restrictions often impose harsher and longer lasting penalties than the original sentence did.

Unfortunately, since these legal consequences are not part of the formal sentencing process, defendants, defense lawyers, and judges may not even think about them at the time of sentencing. The result is that many criminal defendants plead guilty to criminal offenses without any awareness of the serious financial consequences that later result from these legal restrictions, which will affect both their own future daily life and their families.

There also may be barriers to accessing the safety net provided by many social service programs, most needed when ex-offenders are first released."[29] Thus, the consequences of a

---

[29] Kate Adamson, Flynn Carey, Jean Nash, Ryan Flynn, Josh Baker, Rimal Popat, "Collateral Consequences of Criminal Conviction in Arizona," Preliminary Discussion Draft, AZCCStudy8.9.2005.pdf

person's conviction are severe for the vast majority of families of ex-convicts, who consequently struggle mightily to re-establish themselves in society.

The process is equally hard on the families of defendants who plead guilty to a lesser crime, in the false belief that this plea provides an easy way out of the criminal justice system. However, this plea often places them into an even more vulnerable position due to the denial of many benefits they might otherwise receive. For example, ex-cons are prohibited from getting a commercial driver's license, possessing a firearm, and even voting, and a convicted parent may find it more difficult to obtain joint custody after a divorce.[29]

Damage to the Children

Children are especially affected by the incarceration of a parent, since many of them suffer long-lasting negative outcomes related to their health, academic achievement, and behavior. While it may be financially and emotionally advantageous for spouses to break up with the prisoner, many children may be further hurt and traumatized if they have little to no contact with their incarcerated parent. Minority, and particularly black, families are disproportionately affected in this way, because their rates of incarcerated family members are so high.

According to *Prisoners Once Removed*,[28] the ways the children are impacted include:

❖ Children experience the loss of a parent as a traumatic event, and they suffer under the stigma of having a parent in prison, bearing it as a badge of shame and withdrawing from most social relationships.

❖ Children frequently are unable to cope with their father's incarceration, and they express their feelings of fear, anxiety, and anger by doing badly at school (they are twice as likely to drop out if their father is not present) and by engaging in anti-social behavior, such as stealing and starting fires.

❖ Just as the partner of the incarcerated prisoner may become depressed, children of depressed parents are eight times more likely to become depressed, and to remain that way into adulthood!

❖ Children typically find visits to a prison unpleasant, which further strains family ties by providing negative incentives to visit.

❖ In addition, 40% of the 10 to 17 year-old adolescent children of incarcerated parents often exhibit conduct problems which are predictive of future adult criminality. As researchers have found, "the chances that a young man will engage in criminal activity doubles if he is raised without a father."[30]

❖ Some relevant statistics include the following:
   o 2% of all minor children have a parent in prison;[31]

---

[30] Stop Abusive and Violent Environments study, "How False Allegations Harm Families and Children", p. 6.
[31] Second Chance Coalition Principle, "Families with Incarcerated Parents Fact Sheet"

- during the first four months of a father's absence, the chances that the child's family will fall below the poverty line doubles from 18.5% to 37.5%;[28]
- less than 3% of the children of incarcerated parents go to college compared to 39.6% of others;[32]
- in 2012, 51% of 16-19 year-old children of incarcerated parents were unemployed compared to 23.7% of those in the general population.[33]

❖ Children of incarcerated parents are more likely to experience family and residential instability, and they end up in the foster care system more often than other children.[31]

[32] Pew Social and Demographic Trends, Pew Research Center, "College Enrollment Hits an All Time High, Fueled by Community College Surge", http://www.pewsocialtrends.org/2009/10/29/college-enrollment-hits-all-time-high-fueled-by-community-college-surge

[33] Bureau of Labor Statistics, Table 1A. Employment status of the civilian population by sex and age, http://www.bls.gov/news.release.empsit.t01.htm

Suggested Solutions

What can be done to alleviate the real burden and hurts families of convicted defendants face? I suggest:

➤ New sentencing policies could be put in place for nonviolent offenders with families to keep them out of prison or provide a shortened prison term. This could involve sentencing them to participate in community-based work-related programs that permit offenders with families to live at home or visit children on a regular basis. Another possibility might involve using community volunteer credits to offset a sentence, and imposing a suspended sentence that only results in imprisonment if the offender offends again.

➤ Extra counseling, tutoring, and mentoring support through schools could be provided to children of incarcerated parents. This extra social assistance could help head off the likely problems of poor school performance and bad behavior. Group counseling could help these kids know that they're not alone.

➤ Support programs might be provided for the wives and children of returning prisoners, much like the programs provided for families of returning soldiers, to help them better know what difficulties to expect. If family members are informed about any potential employment or licensing difficulties the ex-prisoner might face in advance, they can better help the formerly incarcerated parent adjust to these new realities.

➤ Expansion of re-entry and job training for prisoners and ex-prisoners to help them successfully re-enter normal society. Such training might include help with finding jobs, acquiring new skills or updating old ones, and placement programs to tutor prisoners so they perform better in job interviews and advise them about searching websites such as www.indeed.com. It might also provide support groups for prisoners re-entering society, so they can share their experiences.

➤ New prison parenting programs could be offered to help prisoners remain in good contact with their children; still other programs might be created to help ex-prisoners return to parenting and re-establish a good, solid relationship with their children upon their return.

➤ Community-based agencies, such as volunteer and faith-based organizations, should be invited to provide prisoners and ex-convicts with institutional job-skills programs. For example, Project Return,[34] a community-inspired project started by five ministers in Nashville as a 501 (c)(3) Nonprofit Organization, offers pre-release and job-readiness classes. Additionally, it offers some post-conviction programs, including the following:
  o housing referrals,
  o emergency food boxes,
  o purchasing and providing work tools,
  o transportation through metro Nashville transit bus passes,

---

[34] http://www.projectreturninc.org/about/index.html

- clothing referrals, such as to the Salvation Army and Dress for Success),
- medical referrals, such as for treatment for substance abuse and mental health issues,
- assistance with securing birth certificates, ID cards, and Social Security cards.

Such programs offered by these agencies would likely be much better coordinated than by programs offered by federal or state bureaucracies, where turf wars often result in a redundancy of effort and little effective coordination.

➢ Create a path to reduce the automatic licensing restrictions that limit the jobs ex-cons can take without jeopardizing the rights of employers. For example, on a case-by-case basis, ex-cons could apply for an exemption whereby they can submit letters of recommendations to remove their restriction on a provisional basis, while letting the employer know this restriction has been removed. After six months of successfully performing the work subject to the restrictive license, the restriction could be removed permanently, unless the ex-con is convicted for another crime.

CHAPTER 3: POLICE ISSUES

The first encounters of those who wind up in jail or prison are with police. For years blacks have complained about being profiled by police, but the past few years have been marked by an increased perception by liberals that the police are killing more and more unarmed blacks. This has sparked protests led by black lawmakers and fanned by the Black Lives Matter movement. In some instances, this perception has led to a breakdown of law and order in the form of riots and looting. Although these reactions have not been as severe as the riots in Newark, Watts or Detroit in the 1960s, a second horrendous phenomenon has appeared recently: ambush killings of police engaged in ordinary day-to-day activities. Let's consider these issues one at a time.

Complaints of Misconduct by the Police

Killings by police are frequently lumped together with other serious accusations into a category termed "misconduct complaints." Police operate under great stress, and their lives are often at risk. Thus, it should not be surprising if some participate in misconduct. Only about 1% of police officers are subject to misconduct complaints, though it is difficult to obtain accurate statistics, since neither the government nor police agencies regularly collect such data. However, some "cop watch" groups do. The libertarian Cato Institute's National Police Misconduct Reporting Project's 2010 report[35]

---

[35] David Packman, "Putting Police Misconduct Statistics in Perspective," *The Cato Institute's Project*, October 28, 2009,

cited 4,861 reports of police misconduct throughout the nation. Only 33% of the criminal cases brought against these police officers resulted in convictions, with 36% of those convictions resulting in incarcerations. These statistics suggest that most misconduct claims were unfounded, although some groups claim that these failures to convict were because the officers were protected by the powers that be. Statistical results can often be interpreted differently

In this case, the Cato Project report ultimately concluded that, even though most of the charges against police were unfounded, the police are more likely than the average person to commit a number of crimes, among them assault, sexual assault and murder. They estimated that about 1 in 4.7 officers will be involved in some act of misconduct during their careers.[36]

Misconduct may go unreported and thus be underestimated for two reasons. First, is the "police code of silence," whereby individual officers will not turn each other in, even if they observe another officer behaving badly. Second, many victims of police abuse don't file complaints.

On the other hand, many claims of misconduct may be overblown, brought by individuals with their own agenda to discredit the police. Certain police actions might be justified under the circumstances, but they can be blown up into the police acting wrongly. An example might be where a police officer stops a motorist for what is just a routine traffic infraction. But then the citizen becomes hostile or looks like he is reaching for a gun, leading a police officer to make a

---

http://www.policemisconduct.net/putting-police-misconduct-statistics-in-perspective

[36] David Packman, "Putting Police Misconduct Statistics in Perspective," *The Cato Institute's Project*, October 28, 2009, http://www.policemisconduct.net/putting-police-misconduct-statistics-in-perspective

split second decision to protect his or her own life. Such cases can be quickly turned into both a liberal attack on the police officer for committing murder and the police department for protecting the officer from the charge. In such cases, it is important to look critically at the nature of the encounter to determine who is really at fault -- or if the shooting is due to uncertain actions on both sides. Such uncertainty could mean the case is more of a tragic accident based on misperception and miscommunications.

On the other hand, misconduct can be more widespread than just involving an individual police officer. One of the most famous cases of police misconduct happened back in the late 1990s. At that time, more than seventy LAPD officers assigned to the Rampart Division with the Community Resources Against Street Hoodlums (CRASH) anti-gang unit were implicated in some form of misconduct. Among these were "unprovoked shootings, unprovoked beatings, planting of false evidence, framing of suspects, sealing and dealing narcotics, bank robbery, perjury, and covering up of evidence of these activities."[37,38]

Eventually, fifty-eight officers were brought before an internal administrative board, but only twenty-four were found to have actually engaged in wrongdoing — and of these, twelve were given suspensions of various lengths, seven resigned or retired, and five were fired. Still, the repercussions were huge. Because of falsified evidence and police perjury, 106 prior criminal convictions were overturned and more than 140 civil lawsuits were filed

---

[37] S.E. Smith, "What was the Rampart scandal?" *WiseGeek*, http://www.wisegeek.com/what-was-the-rampart-scandal.htm
[38] Renford Reese, "The Multiple Causes of the LAPD Rampart Scandal," California State Polytechnic Institute, Pomona, California, Fall, 2003, http://www.csupomona.edu/~jis/2003/Reese.pdf

against the city of Los Angeles costing the city about $125 million in settlements.[39] Fortunately, since that time, the LAPD has undergone much reform under Chief William Bratton, who subsequently became the NYPD Commissioner, reducing both police misconduct and consequent claims of misconduct.

Two Major Laws that Can Be Abused

Two major laws are designed to facilitate communications between the police and citizens who seem suspicious, or whose actions give rise to a belief they may have illegal property or weapons. These laws can help the police better know how to handle a situation to cool things down or effect a valid arrest with a citizen who really does have illegal property or weapons. However, the police can take unfair advantage of these laws, and liberals do accuse them of misuse of the laws.

Stop and Identify

The stop-and-identify laws are statutes that allow the police to detain people and ask them to identify themselves, commonly by showing an ID. If the individuals refuse to properly identify themselves or show a false ID, the police are in their rights to arrest them. However, if a police officer simply stops to chat with someone for just a "contact" or "conversation," that person is free to not respond, or leave the conversation. Should the police decide that a person they are

---

[39] CNN Justice, "Ex-L.A. cop sentenced to 5 years," August 7, 2002, http://articles.cnn.com/2002-08-07/justice/rampart.sentencing_1_corruption-scandal-officer-nino-durden-police-officer?_s=PM:LAW

talking to is not free to go, such a conversation/contact becomes "a detention" — and that is when the laws about stop and identify (and arrest) come into play. An example of when a police officer might justifiably turn a chat into a detention is when the conversation leads the officer to suspect the citizen has been involved in a crime.

A common problem is that citizens can be confused about when a conversation ends and a detention begins, since at any time a police officer can approach a person to ask them questions. For example: An encounter may begin if the officer suspects someone is involved in a crime, but does not yet possess the "specific and articulable facts" that could justify that person's detention or arrest. The criteria that need to be met to justify a detention are vague, and so the police are often able to claim the right to question based on ambiguous "facts" — facts that could fit nearly any person in the area as their criteria! Consider, for example, if the police are using a description of a suspect as "a tall African-American male" as the basis for their questioning, and yet this "fact" could fit nearly any male living or walking in the area. This then can result in racial profiling. On the other hand, if a shop owner has reported that a tall African-American male just held him up, then a police officer might be justified in holding a tall black male found within a few blocks of the store for questioning, since he is close enough to have committed that crime. Such a detention might be fully reasonable under the circumstances in this case.

The original statutes about detention go back to Terry v. Ohio.[40] It gave local and state police the ability to briefly detain a person if they have a "...reasonable suspicion that the person has committed, is committing, or is about to commit a crime." Under Terry, the police can conduct a limited search

---

[40]392 U.S. 1, https://supreme.justia.com/us/392/1/case.html (1968)

for weapons (a "frisk") if they reasonably suspect that the person to be detained may be armed and dangerous.[41]

Abuse occurs when police officers use the laws covering detention in conjunction with racial profiling, or with targeting people who live in an area known for a high rate of crime. Here, the police may not have any specific information that a particular person is involved in a crime, but they still may stop that person on the street anytime for questioning. In fact, it has become commonplace nowadays that police frequently detain those living in inner city areas for such questioning, perhaps up to several times a day. Mere failure to identify oneself can merit jail time up to a year or steep fines in certain jurisdictions.[42] On the other hand, if a police officer reasonably suspects that an individual matches a description of a suspect in a crime, he can reasonably detain that person and if further questioning or evidence supports this suspicion, the officer is justified in making an arrest.

Liberals often claim that abuse occurs in those cities and states where there is a large Hispanic population, and police are using the stop-and-identify laws in order to check and see if a person is an illegal immigrant. If the person is, the police then may turn the individual over to the Immigration and Naturalization Service (INS). Under the Trump administration, this has led to confrontation between the federal government and so-called Sanctuary Cities, where local government has instructed police not to cooperate with the INS.

---

[41] Laura Scarry, "Stop & Identify: Can an Officer Arrest a Suspect for Failing to Provide ID?", *Law Officer Magazine*, October 27, 2005; http://www.policeone.com/columnists/lom/articles/120321-Stop-Identify-Can-an-officer-arrest-a-suspect-for-failing-to-produce-ID

[42] Clay White, "Failure to Identify to a Police Officer: Laws and Penalties", *Criminal Defense Lawyer.com*; http://www.criminaldefenselawyer.com/crime-penalties/federal/Failure-identify-police-officer.htm

In other areas, the police might be using the stop-and-identify laws to target someone believed to be on parole or probation to investigate them further — even if the individual is not doing anything illegal at that specific point — and then find a reason to make an arrest. A scathing report was recently issued on the Ferguson, Missouri police force by the Obama administration Department of Justice for civil offenses of this sort against blacks.[43] Still, in many cases, a police officer is justified in using these stop-and-identify laws when the individual on parole or probation is in the area where a crime has just occurred and matches the description of the perpetrator.

In short, liberals claim that police officers have used and are using the stop- and-identify laws to target and harass a particular individual or class of defendants based on racial profiling, given the discretion of the police to interpret terms such as "reasonable suspicion," "probable cause," and "articulable facts." But for the reasons previously noted, citizens' claims of being targeted and harassed might be exaggerated or mistaken, so it is important to look at the circumstances of each case to determine if a detention or arrest was really warranted or not.

Search and Seizure

There is also a potential for police misconduct when a detention turns into an arrest. While the standard for a detention is a reasonable suspicion that a person is involved or may be involved in criminal activity, an arrest requires probable cause, or "enough reliable information" to "support

---

[43] http://apps.washingtonpost.com/g/documents/national/department-of-justice-report-on-the-ferguson-mo-police-department/1435

a reasonable belief that a person has committed a crime." When an arrest occurs, the police now are able to search a person as well their belongings and immediate surroundings.

If police have insufficient evidence, they may be tempted to arrest a person without probable cause, which then allows them to search for more evidence, albeit illegally. If the person arrested hires an attorney afterwards, the lawyer could claim the search was illegal, which could result in the evidence thrown out. Yet many times those arrested who have a low-income status cannot afford to hire a lawyer to file such a motion. In turn, a suspect's inability to hire a lawyer could tempt police to take advantage of technically illegal loopholes in order to better keep our streets safe. At the same time, this permission to search for more evidence can be justified in many cases, if the information the police officer gets from the initial questioning suggests the individual questioned is likely to be involved in a recently committed crime.

Based on the Fourth Amendment, the police are not allowed to unreasonably seize people or their property. They should not act on a hunch, pretext, or hope they will catch a criminal. They must have reliable information. They must have probable cause,[44] as defined earlier.

A police officer can conduct a search with or without a warrant. To obtain a warrant, the officer needs probable cause and must make a statement signed under oath to the judge in which they state the facts. Then, the search must be made within the boundaries of the search warrant.[44] For example, if the warrant provides a right to search a suspect's garage, it does not give the police the right to also search the suspect's

---

[44]Rich Stim, "Overview of Search and Seizure Laws," *CriminalDefenseLawyer.com*, http://www.criminaldefenselawyer.com/resources/criminal-defense-case/overview-search-and-seizure-laws.htm

house (although the police might uncover evidence that gives them probable cause to search other areas).

Searches can also take place without a warrant, which is where the potential for abuse comes into play. At times, many officers may be unjustifiably accused of abuse when they are only conducting a search as the law allows. However, sometimes anti-police advocates are not familiar with the law when they make these accusations of misconduct against the police. So here are the circumstances in which an officer can justifiably seek more information after stopping a person:

❖ If a police officer makes a legitimate arrest, the officer can make a search "incident to arrest" of both the suspect and the immediate area around the suspect.

❖ If a police officer sees evidence of a crime or illegal contraband in plain view from an area where a police officer already has a right to be, the officer can seize it.

❖ If there is an urgent situation — such as a strong possibility the evidence of a crime will be destroyed or a suspect will escape — then an officer is permitted to conduct a warrantless search.

On face value, these laws seem reasonable. But police officers can be tempted to stretch the definitions and descriptions in these laws to search and seize just about anything. Those subjected to these policies have little recourse, since they are already detained, arrested, or have provided consent (albeit reluctantly). Moreover, illegal searches can only be challenged in the future by attorneys — whom, again, many defendants cannot afford to hire.

Frequently, arrested suspects, their lawyers, or others opposed to the police claim an illegal arrest. If the defendant and police subsequently offer different accounts of what transpired, judges and juries are inclined to believe the officer.

The reality is that such complaints of perceived police misconduct primarily take place in the inner cities, as a police department in a lower-income area of a city may not respect the rights of local citizens whom they may perceive as part of a culture of crime. Conversely, citizens in those areas may be quick to complain of misconduct when the police make an arrest, given the combative nature of police-citizen relationships in the inner cities. In contrast, a police department in the suburbs that deals primarily with middle and upper-income individuals is more likely to be more respectful to its citizens, who can more easily afford to hire lawyers if misconduct occurs. Citizens in the suburbs are also more likely to be willing to give a police officer the benefit of the doubt in these situations that give rise to misconduct claims.

Incentives for Police Misconduct

Arrests and convictions prove particularly easy in inner city neighborhoods where drugs are openly bought and sold on the streets. One reason police target minorities in these areas is that they are rewarded by both pay and promotions based on the numbers of arrests and convictions they make. Also, individuals in these areas, who are more likely to be involved in both selling and buying drugs, are more likely to be members of minority groups. While such arrests may be justified, consider that it is far easier to make arrests that lead to convictions or pleas in drug possession cases than in murder cases, which require substantially more investigative efforts.[45]

Such incentives to make arrests to better secure convictions can contribute to police misconduct. While many police departments have citizen police review boards where individuals can bring complaints, the complaints can be hard to prove when they are basically "he said/she said" cases in which the word of one officer is pitted against the word of a private individual. Commonly, the word of the officer will be given greater credence, even when the individual makes a strong case for a wrongful police action. Thus, here, too, it is important to look at the circumstances of each case to determine if a misconduct case is valid or not. Sometimes misconduct cases really should be dismissed; at other times they should not.

Is there Effective Recourse against Police Misconduct?

It is important to understand the laws about police misconduct and the recourse when it occurs in order to recognize when these laws are properly used, or when claims are employed to further an anti-police agenda. Certainly, police misconduct should be met with appropriate penalties in order to preserve the public trust in the police department. But at other times, these claims against the police can be a basis for undermining the police and should be recognized and rejected.

---

[45]Independent Lens, 4/8/13

At the Federal Level

Federal laws enable a person to file a complaint against police with the U.S. Department of Justice (DOJ), but there are severe limitations.

Typically, criminal and civil cases are investigated and handled separately, even if they arise out of the same incident. In a criminal case, the DOJ brings a case against the accused person in order to punish that person — something that requires a higher standard of evidence. While the DOJ does not function as a victim's lawyer, it may call the victim as a witness in the rare event it decides to prosecute.

By contrast, in a civil case, the DOJ brings its case through litigation or through conducting an administrative investigation against a government authority or law enforcement agency. In such civil suits, the DOJ "seeks to correct a law enforcement agency's policies and practices that fostered the misconduct." Sometimes, there will be additional relief awarded to one or more victims of the misconduct. However, a single incident of misconduct is not enough to bring a case, for it must be part of a "pattern or practice," as recently shown in the DOJ report on Ferguson, Missouri.[46] The DOJ has to show in court that "the agency has an unlawful policy or that the incidents constituted a pattern of unlawful conduct."

The main remedy under this law is to secure injunctive relief to end the misconduct and change the agency's policies and procedures that resulted in or allowed it to occur. There is no provision for the victims of the misconduct to receive any personal monetary relief, and the victim cannot initiate any litigation under this law.

---

[46] http://apps.washingtonpost.com/g/documents/national/department-of-justice-report-on-the-ferguson-mo-police-department/1435

The DOJ typically has a high conviction rate in any cases it brings against citizens, but only a few of the police misconduct cases make it through the DOJ review process. For example, of 10,129 cases the DOJ reviewed, only 2,619 were investigated. Only 79 civil rights cases were filed, of which only 22 were official misconduct cases, including for police abuse.[47] This means less than 0.2% of the more than ten thousand civil cases reviewed resulted in official misconduct cases filed for prosecution.

Not only are police misconduct cases prosecuted at the lowest rate among civil rights prosecutions, but civil rights offenses also are prosecuted less than any other category of offense handled by the U.S. Justice Department.[48] Liberals claim this lack of prosecution could be due to bias against such misconduct prosecutions in order to support the police, even when officers are engaged in misconduct. However, this failure to prosecute could simply reflect current priorities given limitations in budget and staffing for taking on all cases, so that other cases, such as those involving violent crimes, are given a higher priority. Or the agencies involved in these cases could lack sufficient information provided in a timely fashion, so they don't have the ability to prosecute these cases. While there are many reasons for the lack of prosecution, there are two main factors behind the low rate of prosecutions.

First, only a small number of attorneys work in the DOJ's Civil Rights Division. Out of the 9,168 attorneys employed by the DOJ in 1997, there were only 32 full-time attorneys in the Criminal Section of the Civil Rights Division

[47]http://www.columbia.edu/itc/journalism/cases/katrina/Human_Rights_Watch/u spoht ml/uspo34.htm
[48]http://www.columbia.edu/itc/journalism/cases/katrina/Human_Rights_Watch/u spoht ml/uspo34.htm

— the office responsible for prosecuting police and other official misconduct cases.[48]

The second factor is that DOJ prosecutors rely on the FBI to conduct inquiries into allegations of criminal civil rights violations. However, the typical FBI investigation of police abuse complaints is limited to information provided by the local law enforcement agency, and such information may be "routinely inadequate or biased." Moreover, since DOJ rules require that the preliminary FBI report be submitted within a mere twenty-one days, the short deadline reduces the likelihood the FBI has enough time to conduct a thorough investigation.[49] The end result is that the DOJ cannot effectively and efficiently prosecute police misconduct cases.

At the State and Local Level

Few misconduct cases are pursued at the state or local level either, though citizens can file a misconduct complaint to police departments' internal affairs division or to their local community police review board. However, such review boards tend to be overwhelmed with cases of police misconduct. As a result, the boards are often behind on reviewing the cases submitted to them, and consequently only deal with a small percentage of cases. By the time a review panel brings up a case for review at a public hearing, the original complainant may have lost interest in pursuing the matter or has moved elsewhere, and a large percentage of cases are closed without review. Then, too, many of these boards operate in opposition to police groups like the local police union, so often the officers cited do not show up for the

---

[49]http://www.columbia.edu/itc/journalism/cases/katrina/Human_Rights_Watch/u spoht ml/uspo34.htm

hearing(s), which results in postponements. Consequently, a complainant who initially appears for a hearing may lose interest in showing up again. Liberals often cite such delays or dropped cases as evidence of cover-ups of misconduct, and they point to these as barriers to bringing a legitimate misconduct case; but these hurdles to bringing a case also serve as barriers to specious misconduct claims.

Police Brutality and Killings

Unfortunately, claims about police brutality have added to the conflict over whether there is misconduct or not. As a steadfast supporter of law and order, President Trump has made statements recently condoning some aspects of police brutality as part of his stance to have police show criminals who is boss. In response, a number of police chiefs have issued statements objecting to his attitude as counterproductive to community relations.[50]

These police chiefs may well be right, since police brutality can be an example of police misconduct, particularly if the civilians involved die. However, in many cases the arrested citizens trigger a forceful police response because of their own resistance. As a result, there can be extenuating circumstances in what seems like a case of police misconduct. Firing a gun and killing a suspect can occur because the police officer believes his or her life is truly threatened, and the shooting is a matter of life and death. Again, a careful consideration of all the evidence in the case is required, and it may be that a jury gets information not available at the time

---

[50] Brian M. Rosenthal, *Police Criticize Trump for Urging Officers Not to Be 'Too Nice' in Handling Suspects*, New York Times, 7/30/2017.

to the average citizen. So what might seem like a jury whitewash of a police defendant could be due to a more critical jury analysis based on additional facts of the case not known to the general public.

There have been many recent examples of well publicized claims of police brutality, such as the case of Eric Garner, who died as a result of a chokehold by a police officer,[51] the case of Freddie Gray in Baltimore, and even more recent shootings of unarmed civilians in Ferguson, North Charleston, Cleveland and Minneapolis, among others. All these cases resulted in black deaths at the hands of police and prompted serious protests which erupted again in cases where the police subsequently were acquitted of murder, manslaughter or misconduct.

I have addressed this issue of accusations against the police separately in other books. In *The Price of Justice*, I pointed out that the number of such incidents, while regrettable, is still very small compared to the number of blacks who are killed by other blacks. The Black Lives Matter movement might save more black lives by concentrating on what to do about the more numerous black-on-black killings in addition or instead of the less numerous black killings by police. In *Cops Aren't Such Bad Guys*, I pointed out that police are most often justified in the use of deadly force by the terminology in local use of force statutes and in their local specific training on how to respond in escalating confrontation with citizens when they feel their own life is threatened. Additionally, I pointed out in the same book that the public does not appreciate how much the lives and careers of officers involved in such incidents are shredded by

---

[51] http://www.theguardian.com/us-news/video/2014/dec/04/i-cant-breathe-eric-garner-chokehold-death-video

additional civil court proceedings, legal costs, and public disapproval.

Breakdown of Law and Order: Killings of Police and Riots

A truly horrendous development is the recent killings of police in ambush attacks. In at least one case in Dallas, this attack may have been motivated by black anger over unarmed blacks killed by police. Such ambushes strike fear into the hearts of our police protectors and cause them to approach situations as tense as car stops with a sense that their lives are in danger. That in turn may have led to more blacks killed by police acting in fear of their lives. Thus, confrontations between police and blacks are growing ever more dangerous and need to be approached with new guidelines.

Similarly, protests by black communities over the loss of their members to police action are increasingly leading to riots and looting, which generally hurt the black communities where these incidents most often occur. In these cases, public sentiment is often revved up by the media eager to cover any confrontations live, which makes such confrontations even more likely to occur. The liberal media coverage of these confrontations has been growing ever more biased against the police since President Trump took office. Blacks and liberals have mobilized to speak out in more and more caustic, divisive terms. With each protest confrontation, the danger increases that some young African-American will want to show off by confronting the police violently. And then there are the white supremacist, neo-Nazi baiting incidents of college students in Charlottesville and Berkeley.

With the social media helping both sides share information and coordinate these protests, we grow increasingly closer to the brink of all-out race riots around the country of the sort that occurred in the 1960s or even more widespread ones. Cooler heads must prevail if we are to head those off.

Photography of Police Actions

Often, the public collects and reveals evidence of police misconduct and abuse through video and audio recordings that provide a record of what really happened in instances of alleged police misconduct. At the same time, in many cases, the police are recording these incidents from their car videos or body cams, and these sometimes show that the police action was justified. So again, a careful review of what happened in each case is needed to make a fair conclusion about whether there was misconduct or not.

For example, there was a video taken of the in-the-back shooting of citizen Oscar Grant at an Oakland, CA station, which was featured in the recent movie *Fruitvale Station*. Eventually, Bay Area Rapid Transit (BART) Officer Mehserle, who claimed he had mistakenly drawn his gun instead of a Taser, was found guilty of involuntary manslaughter, and BART settled with the mother of Grant's daughter for $1.5 million.[52] A more recent example is the Eric Garner case in New York, in which Garner was asphyxiated in a chokehold when a police offer held him down while

---

[52] Demian Bulwa, "BART Pays $1.5 Million to Aid Grant's Daughter, *SF Gate, San Francisco Chronicle*, January 28, 2010, http://www.sfgate.com/bayarea/article/BART-pays-1-5-million-to-aid-Grant-s-daughter-3201450.php

trying to make an arrest.[53] Though Garner repeated said: "I can't breathe," the officer continued the hold until Garner finally died.

In response to the growing use of digital recording devices by the public, usually used to show misconduct, for a time there was a police backlash — resulting in the police recording the citizens recording them. Even though such recordings are usually legal under the free speech provisions of the 1st amendment if the citizen is standing on public grounds, the police used eavesdropping and wiretapping laws to charge citizens who recorded them without their knowledge.

In other cases, police may have illegally confiscated cameras, deleted evidence, or incorrectly told citizens they are not allowed to film. However, when citizens were able to record and keep their audios or videos, even surreptitiously, these records of what really happened have played an important role in making the public aware of police misconduct. The video recording of the police shooting of Walter Scott in North Charleston, S.C. in 2015, resulting in a murder charge against the police officer and a mistrial,[54] is one such incident. Lately, the police have adopted a less confrontational posture toward citizens recording their action, by letting citizens freely record these encounters.

In like fashion, many police departments are now recording more incidents themselves with cameras mounted on officers or police cars. They find that this reduces the incidence of misconduct, since the police become more careful to conform to the law. Most importantly, these

---

[53]http://www.theguardian.com/us-news/video/2014/dec/04/i-cant-breathe-eric-garner-chokehold-death-video

[54] https://www.nytimes.com/2016/12/05/us/walter-scott-michael-slager-north-charleston.html

recordings provide evidence justifying police action in most incidents. Thus, these recordings help to keep both sides more honest in revealing misconduct when it occurs and when it does not.

Suggested Solutions

We need to continue supporting our police. However, some suggestions to reduce the relatively few abuses by the police include the following:

> Create a national clearinghouse for reports by citizen-police review boards. Members of Congress could introduce legislation to fund this organization. The organization could review any complaints in a timely fashion and provide a national record of complaints that could be accessed by citizens everywhere. Such a database would keep police misconduct from being "buried" in local files, so people could know the real extent of misconduct, rather than depending on the claims made to support dueling political agendas.

> Develop national training guidelines and policies for police departments nationwide—a "code of conduct" that local police departments could follow in order to improve police operations, increase compliance, and reduce citizen complaints against the police. The clearinghouse described above could facilitate this.

> Local citizen review boards could include some members of the local board of supervisors (a governing body in many cities composed of representatives chosen by district or citywide elections). Increasing citizen involvement on these boards would improve awareness and accountability. With little community-wide participation present in these boards as of this writing, the boards are often ignored by the police department internal affairs

divisions, which tend to support the police version of events and are influenced by the police "code of silence." More community support and awareness of these review boards might come about through more outreach to the local communities, such as by establishing a regular column in a local paper or weekly blog. Citizen review boards also might actively search out community leaders to get them involved. For example, board members might promote citizen participation at local business groups, such as the city's Chamber of Commerce.

➢ A training program might be developed to increase police awareness of local community needs and show how officers could better interact with local citizens in a spirit of trust and cooperation. This program might be designed or selected by a team of consultants who already work as advisors to the city's police department. In such a training program, police officers could be shown how to better understand the main types of complaints against them and, where justified, how to change their behavior to reduce such complaints in the future. Alternatively, if these complaints aren't justified, the city might create an outreach educational program to promote more understanding in the community about what the police are permitted to do in the situations that have led to these unjustified complaints.

➢ The Department of Justice could require the FBI to perform its own independent investigations of police misconduct rather than relying on information provided by the police.

➤ The media should be encouraged not to fan the waves of racial indignation with each unfortunate exceptional incident between police and blacks. This sensational news reporting may serve the media with more "Breaking News," but it does not serve the public well, and false claims of misconduct can lead to protests and even riots. The media could serve the public better with more investigative reporting regarding trends in police action and potential abuse.

➤ The police must receive additional training to help prevent racial protests from developing into race riots. That training should involve close cooperation between protest organizers and the police, with the understanding that neither side nor the nation can withstand the consequences of serious race riots. Remember that a thousand police were unable to stop violent confrontations between rival white protestors and predominantly white counter-protestors recently in Charlottesville. Those police who provide security for protests may need to be specially selected or trained not to overreact. Careful consideration has to be given to the advantages and disadvantages of the display of overwhelming force with military-supplied weaponry.

➤ Remove any restrictions on the public in filming and recording the police when they are on duty, except when filming or recording interferes with the officer's duty.

➤ The expanded and mandatory use of new technologies *by police* should be encouraged, such as making audio recordings when a police officer stops or arrests a citizen, and recording videos from small cameras attached to a police officer's uniform. These recordings should prove useful, if there are contradictory accounts by a police officer and a citizen. These recordings will also discourage citizens from filing false claims that they or another citizen were subjected to police misconduct when this did not occur.

CHAPTER 4: POWERFUL PROSECUTORS MISBEHAVING

Prosecutors wield extraordinary power, but just as easily as they can put true criminals behind bars, they can destroy the lives of innocent defendants. Prosecutors are expected to seek truth and justice, and it is important to support prosecutors who are dedicated to those goals. After all, they are part of our defense against the bad guys.

But prosecutors are also saddled with tremendous pressure from supervisors to aggressively pursue convictions or score "winning" plea bargains. Often the push to gain convictions — and the praise that follows a conviction — can overcome the prosecutorial directive to seek what is true and just. So prosecutors selectively choose which cases to prosecute and how, with limited checks on their conduct. A recent 2017 book by John Pfaff even concluded that prosecutors are the single group most responsible for our bloated prison system. This is on account of their successful convictions of low-level criminals involved in non-violent crimes who received harsh prison sentences. Additionally, in many cases they have obtained convictions against defendants who were later found not-guilty.[55]

Since 1997, there have been 201 criminal cases where federal judges determined that select U.S. Department of Justice prosecutors violated laws or ethics rules. Forty-seven of these defendants were exonerated later, with only one federal prosecutor being barred (temporarily) from practicing

---

[55] John F. Pfaff, *Locked In, The True Causes of Mass Incarceration and How to Achieve Real Reform*, Basic Books, 2017.

law for misconduct in the last twelve years.[56] Although more than 700 prosecutors in California committed prosecutorial misconduct between 1997 and 2009, according to state, federal, and appellate court opinions, a Santa Clara University School of Law study noted that the authorities failed to either report or even discipline these prosecutors. The California State Bar disciplined only six of the prosecutors involved.[57]

In a series of lengthy article on prosecutorial misconduct, journalists Ken Armstrong and Maurice Possley of the Chicago Tribune reported, "With impunity, prosecutors across the country have violated their oaths and the law, committing the worst kinds of deception in the most serious of cases... They do it to win. They do it because they won't get punished."[58]

Such kinds of deceptions should not be tolerated, because they undermine the work of prosecutors pursuing the goal of justice, and they threaten support for the vast majority of prosecutors who have the general interests of the public at heart.

What kind of deception were these prosecutors engaged in? As also pointed out by Armstrong and Possley back in 1999, these deceptions include the following:

- ❖ Since a 1963 U.S. Supreme Court ruling designed to curb misconduct by prosecutors, at least 381 defendants nationally have had a homicide conviction

---

[56] Studies: USA Today Investigation Reveals Prosecutorial Misconduct in Federal Cases. http://deathpenaltyinfo.org/studies-usa-today-investigation-reveals-prosecutorial-misconduct-federal-cases

[57] Kathleen Ridolfi and Maurice Possley "Preventable Error: A Report on Prosecutorial Misconduct in California 1997-2009" http://digitalcommons.law.scu.edu/ncippubs/2

[58] *Chicago Tribune*, http://www.chicagotribune.com/news/watchdog/chi-020103trial1,0,479347.story

thrown out, because prosecutors concealed evidence suggesting innocence or presented evidence they knew to be false. … And that number represents only a fraction of how often such cheating occurs."[59]

❖ This small number of cases of prosecutorial misconduct is, in part, because much of the violation of the act is unreported. This lack of reporting occurs since most convicts are impoverished and can't afford representation to adequately fight back against a prosecutor intent on a conviction.[59]

❖ The U.S. Supreme Court declared that misconduct by prosecutors is so reprehensible that it warrants criminal charges and disbarment.[59] But not one of those prosecutors who was charged with misconduct was convicted of a crime. Not one was barred from practicing law. Instead, many saw their careers advance, later to become judges or district attorneys.[59]

There is no indication the situation has improved-since that time. Many of the now-publicized cases of prosecutorial misconduct in convictions incorrectly used DNA evidence to support their cases. Because of this behavior, more than 250 defendants who were convicted of crimes they did not commit have been exonerated — a revelation exposed only as a result of appeals. Barry Scheck of the Innocence Project notes that only a small number of prosecutors have been sanctioned, even when acts of misconduct have led to cases being overturned. As he observed:

"Our system rarely disciplines, much less brings criminal charges against prosecutors who have

---

[59] *Chicago Tribune*, http://www.chicagotribune.com/news/watchdog/chi-020103trial1,0,479347.story

engaged in acts of intentional misconduct. Far too often, prosecutors, who wield enormous power over our lives, aren't investigated at all, even for intentional misconduct that has led to a wrongful conviction, much less 'harmless' intentional misconduct in cases in which the defendant was guilty."[60]

So in what kinds of misbehavior are criminal prosecutors engaged?

Major Types of Prosecutorial Misconduct

[60]http://www.innocenceproject.org/news-events-exonerations/errant-prosecutors-seldom-held-to-account

Playing Politics with Evidence

One of the most common types of prosecutorial misconduct is not providing the defense team with all the evidence the prosecution has gathered, in particular evidence that is exculpatory (favorable to the defendant). While prosecutors are constitutionally obligated to share any evidence favorable to the defendant with the defense, they are essentially immune from prosecution themselves. Consequently, prosecutors often ignore this obligation, either intentionally or through negligence.

An example is a prosecutor who knows that a witness has recanted his or her statement against the defendant or knows that the results of an investigation or crime lab test have undercut their theory of the case. Another example is where the evidence points to the non-existence of a crime, such as when a victim or witness is lying, or when there is evidence the crime actually resulted from an accident; but the prosecutor chooses not to use this evidence, does not show it to the defense, and/or does not close the case.

Worse, a prosecutor may not only downplay or ignore such exculpatory evidence, but in some cases a prosecutor may actively hide or destroy this evidence, or fabricate other evidence to win the case. These serious breaches of the public trust make a mockery of our justice system, and can lead to wrongful convictions or actions against a defendant. While the outcome of a wrongly convicted defendant may be shocking due to the injustice caused by a vengeful or neglectful prosecutor, another result is higher economic costs due to a wrongful incarceration. Not only are there costs of maintaining the convict in prison, but there is the loss of income from a productive citizen. Later lawsuits from defense attorneys may result, too, due to wrongful conviction and imprisonment. Worst of all, the actual perpetrator of the crime may still be at large and committing further crimes.

One high-profile case where the prosecutors concealed evidence to win a case against a high-profile defendant is that of Senator Ted Stevens, a Republican seeking re-election in Alaska. The case revolved around a charge that Stevens had failed to report more than $250,000 in illegal gifts and home renovations received between May 1999 and August 2007. The defendant insisted that he had intended to pay for all of the work performed on his house.

The jury found Stevens guilty of seven felony counts for failing to disclose the renovations and other gifts. A few days after this verdict, Stevens, the longest-serving Republican Senator in history, narrowly lost his re-election bid.

But he wasn't actually guilty and didn't need to drop out or lose the election. Less than a year later, a U.S. District Judge threw out the case at the request of the Justice Department, which found that exculpatory evidence had been withheld at the trial. The judge, Emmet G. Sullivan, took the unprecedented step of appointing a court-appointed special counsel, Henry F. Schuelke III, to investigate the six prosecutors who had handled Stevens' investigation and trial. After a two-year investigation of more than 128,000 pages of documents, Schuelke concluded, "Significant evidence was not disclosed to the defense and critical mistakes were made throughout the course of the trial that denied Senator Stevens a fair opportunity to defend himself." In short, the prosecutors withheld all sorts of materials that would have supported Senator Stevens's contention that he had intended to pay. Thus, the prosecutors had won their conviction through intentionally withholding and concealing evidence, so the guilty verdict was overturned.

While Schuelke stated the two prosecutors' actions were "...broadly illegal," he also said he could not bring criminal contempt charges against the prosecutors who had "intentionally withheld exculpatory information because the judge had not specifically issued an order telling them to turn over such evidence."[61] The prosecutors in question escaped with little punishment aside from an admonition for their bad behavior. And, of course, taxpayers had to foot the bill for what turned out to be a wrongly pursued prosecution.

Ignoring Evidence of a Witness's Lies, and/or Leaking Inflammatory and Prejudicial Information

Prosecutorial misconduct also occurs when a prosecutor improperly relies on the testimony of unreliable witnesses to make a case, or on those with an axe to grind. Or sometimes a prosecutor might rely on the use of "snitches" who are in jail or facing criminal charges. However, snitches are often unreliable witnesses, since they lie to reduce their sentence or to have the charges against them dismissed.

Sometimes prosecutors deliberately reveal prejudicial and inflammatory information to the press to support their personal belief that a defendant is guilty in advance of a trial. This is exactly what a prosecutor did in the notorious Duke University lacrosse team case in which three players were falsely accused of rape. The prosecutorial misconduct was so great in this case that the prosecutor was criminally charged for his crime, disbarred, fined, convicted, and served a short jail sentence.

---

[61] http://www.washingtontimes.com/news/2012/mar/28/senator-prosecutorial-misconduct-stevens-case-cann/?page=all

The case began in March 2006, after the Duke men's lacrosse team held a party at which they had arranged for two strippers to appear to dance for the group. There were some arguments between the men and the strippers during their performance, and shortly before one a.m., the strippers, Crystal Mangum and Kim Roberts, entered a car and drove off. After the two women got into an argument in a parking lot, police took Mangum, an African-American, to the Durham Access Center, a mental-health and substance abuse facility for involuntary commitment. While Mangum was being admitted, she claimed she had been raped in the bathroom at the house by three men, and she was transferred to the Duke University Medical Center for tests. She received treatment there for some genital injuries, but it was unclear that her injuries were consistent with rape.[62]

Although Mangum's story kept changing and vast evidence existed to show she had not been where she claimed to be with the men, prosecutor Mike Nifong proceeded as if this was a slam-dunk case of rape. He did everything in his power to prove it regardless of what the evidence showed, and he sought to make his case in the court of public opinion through media leaks as well as in court. The prosecution ordered the members of the team to provide DNA samples and had them analyzed at two different labs. Though none of these samples was a DNA match with any of the Duke players, the tests showed DNA from multiple males inside Mangum and on her underwear. Even so, Nifong was undeterred by this evidence and continued with the case.

The results of Nifong's charges of first-degree forcible rape, first-degree sexual offense, and kidnapping, along with

---

[62] Stuart Taylor and K.C. Johnson, "Until Proven Innocent: Political Correctness and the Shameful Injustices of the Duke Lacrosse Rape Case", *St. Martin's Griffin*, 2008.

other information he released to the media were devastating to the three defendants charged, as well as to the school. What made the story even more explosive was that the prosecution charged the alleged assault as a hate crime, because the woman was black and the three men were white.

After Nifong framed the issue as race hatred by rich white fraternity boys against minority women, there were threats of gang violence against the general Duke student population. The press stirred up emotions, too, by vilifying the lacrosse team players for their attack on the two women. In effect, Nifong was able to stir up public opinion to ensure that the three men charged with the crime would be considered guilty even before the case went to trial.

Initially, Nifong was able to get away with this misconduct since his false narrative fed into a public perception that high status white frat boys would think they could take advantage of low status black women. However, the public did not know at that time that Mangum, the primary accuser, had a long history of mental problems and had been previously diagnosed with bipolar disorder. Mangum had also made a similar rape claim ten years before in 1995, although she had repeatedly changed her story and had never pursued it. In the Duke case, she also changed her descriptions of the three men who raped her to the police. Moreover, the testimony of the second stripper, Kim Roberts, undermined her claim, since she stated Mangum was not raped.

Despite the obvious flaws in the case, Nifong continued to pursue it for another six months, perhaps because backing down would have undermined his political ambitions. But eventually, Nifong withdrew himself from the case and turned it over to North Carolina Attorney General Roy Cooper. After further investigating the case and seeing the obvious lack of evidence, Cooper dismissed all charges against the three players and further declared that they were innocent. As Cooper stated in making his announcement: "We have no credible evidence that an attack occurred."[63]

Cooper then pursued charges against Nifong, declaring him a "rogue prosecutor." A three-member disciplinary panel found him guilty of numerous acts of prosecutorial misconduct, among them: "fraud, dishonesty, deceit or misrepresentation... making false statements of material fact before a judge... making false statements of material fact before bar investigations, and... lying about withholding exculpatory DNA evidence." In passing judgment, Superior Court Judge W. Osmond Smith III found Nifong in contempt, because Nifong had lied to the court during a hearing the previous September about whether all DNA evidence had been provided to the defense attorneys.[64]

Nifong was disbarred and convicted of criminal contempt for knowingly making false statements during criminal proceedings. His sentence? A day in jail. Although his single day in jail might seem a slap on the wrist given all the havoc Nifong caused, it was one of the few times a prosecutor received any punishment for misconduct. At the time, Nifong's motivation to use the case to run for office was well-concealed. A *New York Times* article later characterized how the case was viewed by many "as a morality play of justice run off the rails by political correctness (i.e.: because of the many people who were all too ready to see this as a hate crime against a black woman) and the political ambitions

---

[63] "Duke Lacrosse Sexual Assault Case," *New York Times*, June 22, 2012, topics.nytimes.com/topics/reference/timestopics/organizations/d/duke_universit y/.../index.html
[64] Falsely-accused Duke Lacrosse Players Seek Millions, Reforms," *EPSN.com*, Sept. 7, 2007, espn.go.com/espn/print?id=3008460&type=story

of Mr. Nifong."[65] The sanctions put on Nifong were truly exceptional; it is extremely rare that prosecutorial misconduct is punished.

So if politics was Nifong's motivation, are there other reasons for prosecutorial misconduct? Why is prosecutorial misconduct so rampant? And what can be done about it, because this not only results in false convictions and imprisonment, but high costs borne by the courts and correctional system. If the defendant is convicted, there are also losses to the economy and destabilization of the convict's family, since he is removed from the local community while in prison.

Motivations for Prosecutorial Misconduct

Sometimes, prosecutors in criminal cases engage in misconduct in order to obtain bogus evidence to convict defendants because they believe the defendants really are guilty. To this end, prosecutors may intentionally plant, lose, or tamper with evidence, improperly coerce or reward witnesses, and/or suppress exculpatory evidence or information.[66]

Other times, outside pressures on what cases to charge can easily sway prosecutors to try one case over another. Prosecutors are liable to succumb to this influence, as they have wide discretion in choosing what cases they want to prosecute.

---

[65]"Duke Lacrosse Sexual Assault Case," *New York Times*, June 22, 2012, topics.nytimes.com/topics/reference/timestopics/organizations/d/duke_universit y/.../index.html

[66] The Stopped Clock, "Fabricated Evidence in Criminal Cases," September 7, 2011, http://the stoppedclock.blogspot.com/2011/09/fabricated-evidence-in-criminal-cases.html

Another common reason, previously mentioned, is that prosecutors are often faced with immense pressure from supervisors to win cases. As a result, despite their affirmative duty to turn over all evidence to the defendant, many do not do so, because they feel pressure to obtain a guilty verdict at all costs.[67] This may not always qualify as "misconduct," since they may appear to be just doing their job in actively pursuing a guilty verdict, although ethically prosecutors are supposed to seek the truth. Yet, in a misguided effort to quickly convict and punish a suspect, prosecutors may fail to pursue the truly guilty criminal, because they have focused on the wrong individual, as a result of ignoring other facts or evidence.

Unfortunately, since there are only very weak sanctions for any misbehavior, prosecutors are largely free to do what they want without fear of any reprisal.[68]

---

[67] Jeff Stanglin, "Prosecutorial Misconduct is a Crime: Attorneys Who Are Guilty Should Be Punished, June 30, 2008, suite101.com/article/prosecutorial-misconduct-is-a-crime-a58867, accessed June 17, 2012

[68] Heather Schoenfeld, "Violated Trust: Conceptualizing Prosecutorial Misconduct," *Journal of Contemporary Criminal Justice*, August 2004, Vol. 21. No. 3, 250-271, Abstract.

Suggested Solutions

Since the power of prosecutors is nearly absolute, and most innocent defendants are seriously "outgunned" by the prosecutors' power, it is important for us to change things. Some recommended changes are the following:

> Perhaps one incentive to generate better prosecutorial conduct might be finding a way to increase the pay for prosecutors, since they are poorly paid compared to most lawyers. With more pay, they may be more willing to focus on the merits of the case and less likely to view getting a guilty verdict irrespective of the merits as a stepping-stone to a higher-level position with more income. When one values something and plans to hold onto it for a long period, one treats it better, and with respect.

> Secondly, just as lawyers need to go back every year or two for refresher classes on ethics, prosecutors should be required to attend a similar program for prosecutors each year to remind them of their sworn duty to pursue the truth.

> Third, we must address the real need for qualified, as opposed to absolute immunity for prosecutors. For more on this suggestion, see Chapter 7.

An Example of a Successful Solution in Action

Such suggestions and others are very doable. To illustrate, here's an example of a successful solution which occurred when a prosecutor sought the truth, rather than expedient resolution of cases.

This successful solution occurred when Texas's Dallas County elected a new District Attorney, Craig Watkins, in 2006. The first-ever African-American elected district attorney in Texas history, Watkins took a very different stance toward criminal prosecutions than his predecessors.

Since Dallas had a questionable record in having more DNA exonerations than any other county in the U.S., Watkins partnered with the Innocence Project of Texas to review hundreds of requests for DNA testing. This partnership gained national attention. In addition, Watkins made other fundamental local changes that affected far more cases by shaking up his office. To do so, he first framed and placed on walls through the office an article of the "Texas Code of Criminal Procedure with this one sentence highlighted: "It shall be the duty of all prosecuting attorneys, including any special prosecutors, not to convict but to see that justice is done." Then, he fired some top-level prosecutors, because they did not adhere to this code. Others left.[69]

Watkins also was guided by the policy expressed in this quotation: "Our success is not going to be based on the number of folks we send to prison or death row. That's just evidence of the failure of the criminal justice system."[69]

In turn, Watkins was praised for his actions by Texas lawyers, such as Mark Donald, who had this to say:

"...(Watkins) delicately balances the traditional role of a prosecutor as community enforcer against the more holistic approach of a prosecutor as community problem-solver. That balance has Watkins one day

---

[69] Mark Donald: Texas Lawyer, A Justice-at-All-Costs Attitude--Impact Player of the Year Craig Watkins, 12-24-2007; www.truthinjustice.org/craig-watkins.htm

issuing a press release announcing he will seek the death penalty against an alleged cop killer and the next day rewarding a prosecutor for initiating a Big Brother program that pairs DA staffers with the children of inmates. It has him one day touting his new absconder unit, which will hunt down the most violent probation violators before they can victimize again, and another day selling his ideas about a community court system so neighborhood elders can punish defendants in such a way that victims will be made whole again."[69]

In response to these policies committed to upholding true justice, voters re-elected Watkins in 2010. Kudos to Watkins—and kudos to those Texas citizens.

CHAPTER 5: JUDICIAL LIMITATIONS AND MISBEHAVIOR

Judges wield an enormous amount of power in the judicial system, though they face a number of limitations.

Judicial Limitations

Judges are not all-powerful Solomons, because their hands are tied by a variety of limitations.

Trials and Plea Bargains

First and foremost, the vast majority of cases -- over 90% -- are decided by plea bargains involving agreements between prosecutors and defense attorneys. Judges play very little role in this process other than to validate the agreements.

Jury trials are quite rare and very time-consuming. Judges play a clear role there. The public is familiar with that from numerous television crime series, but it does not realize how rare jury trials are.

Judges have the most influence in trials in which they make the decision as both judge and jury, but these are also extremely rare.

Judges have an important influence in deciding sentences after a trial, but they are subject to limitations here as well.

Limitations Imposed on Judicial Sentencing

The public's desire to have safe neighborhoods and impose law and order has motivated politicians of all stripes to impose more and more stringent penalties for crime. In many cases state legislators have imposed two forms of sentencing guidelines that strictly limit the latitude of judges in imposing sentences. The two which have received the most attention are mandatory minimum sentences and so-called three strikes laws, many of which have been mandated by propositions on state ballots, notably in liberal California. The former do not permit sentences more lenient than the mandatory minimums. Three strikes laws were intended to restrict the revolving door by which career criminals would serve their time, be released, and then habitually re-offend. Instead, these laws make a third crime, no matter how minor, result in a virtual lifetime sentence for the offender. Once enshrined into law, a judge's power to impose an appropriate sentence is taken away.

Unfortunately, this harsh sentencing applied to a third-strike defendant with a very minor offense can result in an unreasonably high sentence, which proves costly for the criminal justice system and the economy, given the loss of the defendant's possible productivity. An example is a defendant with two early offenses who is caught shoplifting a small item, such as food for his hungry family. The result could be a minimum 10-year sentence, which seems unduly extreme.

Judicial Misbehavior

Although judges do not receive the kind of public attention that prosecutors receive when they behave badly, their misbehavior can prove equally devastating.

The behavioral standards to which judges are supposed to adhere are spelled out in the Code of Judicial Conduct, which is designed to guide judges and candidates for judicial office on how to act, as well as provide a structure against which their conduct can be measured in the case of any complaints. These standards are guided by two central principles: First, judges should treat their judicial office as a "public trust." Second, they should "strive to maintain and enhance the public's confidence in our legal system" — which means they should conduct themselves with the proper decorum both in and outside the courtroom.[70]

Judges cannot allow family, social, or political relationships to influence how they decide a case. Nor should they hear or preside over a case if a conflict of interest exists, which can include a personal relationship with one party or a personal interest in the outcome of the case. Judges must remain impartial. Always. Should that impartiality be in doubt, they should disqualify themselves.

Judges also must avoid any appearance of impropriety, and refrain from giving or receiving any sort of gift, loan, or other favor from a lawyer, witness, or any party to the case. To attest to their independence of influence, judges are required to file financial disclosure statements with the court and state ethics commission.[71]

---

[70] David E. Danda, "Complaints Against Judges," *FindLaw for Legal Professionals*, Jan 1, 2001, library.findlaw.com/2001/Jan/1/129441html
[71] David E. Danda, "Complaints Against Judges," *FindLaw for Legal Professionals*, Jan 1, 2001, library.findlaw.com/2001/Jan/1/129441html

Yet despite the existence of some checks on their conduct, judges can sometimes act in ways that fall short of the standard for the office they hold.

Abuses of Judicial Power

The types of abuses of judicial power include the following -- improper courtroom behavior, showing bias, and otherwise exercising their power to do harm.

Improper Courtroom Behavior

The proper calm, impartial, and respectful behavior normally characteristic of judges has been very much distorted by the presentation of court cases on TV. These courtroom shows feature caricatures of judges like Judge Judy,[72] a former judge who insults and embarrasses whomever she thinks has done wrong. In effect, she treats persons in her courtroom as if they are naughty children who need to be slapped. Such judicial behavior might make for entertaining TV — but it undermines the proper courtroom decorum the public should actually expect of a judge.

There are many way in which today's judges can fall short in the courtroom. Some failings are:

❖ Habitual intemperance, such as having an angry, sarcastic tone in making comments in the court; or insulting, ridiculing, or disparaging counsel, the

---

[72] http://www.judgejudy.com

parties, jurors, or witnesses in a case. Judges should display patience, dignity, and courtesy.[73]

❖ Conduct prejudicial to the administration of justice, such as demonstrating a clear preference for one side or the other (usually the prosecutor), and ruling with a bias toward that side.

Showing Bias

Many judges exhibit a bias in favor of the prosecution. Prosecutors represent the state and the community — which are aligned against the defendant — and judges generally identify with the establishment. Thus, when any defendant goes to court, it is like approaching a dealer with a stacked deck that favors the house.

Judges have numerous options that make it "amazingly easy...to fix the outcome of a trial."[74]

These methods include:

❖ Manipulating the jury selection process to favor the prosecution;

❖ Deciding which witnesses can testify and what testimony they are allowed to provide, which can often limit the defense;

---

[73]Michael Paul Thomas, "Judicial Misconduct: Judges Behaving Badly, *Daily Journal*, www.dailyjournal.com/cle.cfm?show=CLEDisplayArticles&qVersionID=85&eid=821923& evid=1

[74] Hans Sherrer in "The Complicity of Judges in the Generation of Wrongful Convictions," *Northern Kentucky Law Review*, Vol. 30:4j.

❖ Determining the physical and documentary items that can be introduced as evidence, and thereby exclude defense exhibits;

❖ Deciding which objections are sustained or overruled, so that the prosecution has more objections sustained, while the defense has more objections overruled;

❖ Conveying to the jurors that the judge negatively perceives the defendant and defense lawyer by the judge's tone of voice and body language;

❖ Providing the instructions to the jury as to the law and how to apply it to the facts which the judge permits the jurors to see and hear, and interpreting the law or determining which facts to present so as to favor the prosecution;[75]

❖ Improperly sharing privileged information with prosecutors outside the courtroom, either in chambers or during social interactions.

If and when a judge behaves in the ways described above, the defendant is being "judicially sandbagged... the judge's opinions of a person's guilt or innocence can be the primary determinate of a trial's outcome, and not whether the person is actually innocent or guilty."[76] Given these contributions of judicial bias to the courtroom, prosecutors end up more likely to win their cases. To cite Sherrer again:

---

[75] Hans Sherrer in "The Complicity of Judges in the Generation of Wrongful Convictions," *Northern Kentucky Law Review*, Vol. 30:4j.
[76] Hans Sherrer in "The Complicity of Judges in the Generation of Wrongful Convictions," *Northern Kentucky Law Review*, Vol. 30:4j.

"Playing an important role in a judge's subtle manipulation of the proceedings in his/her courtroom is the judge's use of mind control techniques on jurors – the same techniques...used by law enforcement interrogators to extra false confessions from innocent men and women...The use of these insidious techniques...is a significant contributor to wrongful convictions...this power is often used to the detriment of innocent men and women, because a judge can use all the methods and nuances of his craft to steer trial in the direction of concluding in the way he or she has pre-determined it should end."[76]

There have been numerous cases after a trial where the jurors, once free of any judicial pressure, have noted that they arrived at a guilty verdict based on what the judge in effect "told" them to do via tone and/or body language.

The Power to Do Harm

Judges hold a tremendous power to do harm to defendants. For example, from their protected perch, a judge can order the police or sheriff to physically seize and drag a defendant to jail, if he or she declines to comply with a judicial command. By the same token, a judge can have someone thrown into jail for contempt of court if the individual does not show the proper respect.

Yet the aura of civility and decorum that may be present in the courtroom can readily mask the true "horror" judges can inflict on innocent defendants by their pronouncements. Lives can be completely turned around and decimated by the flick of a pen.

The mere fear of the judge's power to influence a jury's decision might lead a defendant to accept a damaging and unfair plea. A jury might be influenced by a judge's negative attitude toward the defendant, or by a judge's unfriendly or unsympathetic reaction to defense witnesses and defense attorney: "Judges are able to communicate their biases to jurors not only by non-verbal facial expressions or gestures, but also by friendly or hostile questioning of prosecution or defense witnesses."[77] So again judges can increase the costs to the system and the economy by their bias favoring the prosecution, which leads to more and longer incarcerations, many of them unfair.

Pressuring Defendants to Take Plea Bargains and Make Guilty Pleas

The vast majority of criminal cases are resolved by plea bargains — without which the criminal justice system could not function, as the courts would be overwhelmed by the vast number of cases in the system. Normally, these bargains are resolved by negotiations between the prosecutor and defense attorney. The more judges become involved, the more the negotiation process can be prejudicial against the defendant.[78]

A key reason judges do get involved is administrative: by encouraging defendants to enter guilty pleas, they can move the court calendar forward. Their involvement can put unwarranted pressure on the defendant, whose own lawyer has a busy caseload, while a prosecutor eager to rack up

---

[77] Richard Klein, "Judicial Misbehavior in Criminal Cases: It's Not Just the Counsel Who May Be Ineffective and Unprofessional," *Ohio State Journal of Criminal Law*, Vol 4: 195, 2006.

[78] Richard Klein, "Judicial Misbehavior in Criminal Cases: It's Not Just the Counsel Who May Be Ineffective and Unprofessional," *Ohio State Journal of Criminal Law*, Vol 4: 195, 2006.

another win might already be encouraging the defendant to plead. Such a plea may not be in the defendant's best interest though, so if the judge applies additional pressure on the defendant, it undermines the judge's impartiality in the case, and combined with the defense attorney push to settle, can lead to the defendant agreeing to the plea. Such a plea is akin to a litigant accepting a bad deal, when facing the power of expensive lawyers on the opposing side and an overburdened attorney who wants the case to settle quickly at any cost.

When the defense attorney and prosecutor are unable to obtain a plea bargain, the judge may put pressure on the defendant to enter a guilty plea. Commonly, the judge views the defendant as the "recalcitrant party" and so applies this pressure to "get rid of" the case.[78] To this end, this pressure can involve telling a defendant that if he or she does not enter a guilty plea that day, the judge will not impose a favorable sentence in the future. For instance, the judge might say something like this to a defendant: "This is a one-time offer;" "This offer is for today only;" or "I'll make sure you get sentenced to the max, if you don't plead guilty now." Or, a judge might advise the defense counsel thusly: "I strongly suggest that you ask your client to consider a plea, because if the jury returns a verdict of guilty, I might be disposed to impose a substantial prison sentence."[79]

In one Supreme Court of New York case, the judge told a defendant if he refused the offered plea and went to trial, he would make sure the defendant would be "sentenced to the maximum time of incarceration permitted by law."[79] In another particularly horrifying New York case, the presiding judge was adamant that the teenage male defendant accept a

---

[79] Richard Klein, "Judicial Misbehavior in Criminal Cases: It's Not Just the Counsel Who May Be Ineffective and Unprofessional," *Ohio State Journal of Criminal Law*, Vol 4: 195, 2006.

plea, although the defendant kept refusing to plead guilty. In his last words to the judge, the defendant said, "I'm nineteen-years-old, Your Honor. That is terrible. That's terrible." The defendant then turned to face his weeping mother and said, "Mom, I can't do it," before jumping out the sixteenth-floor-courtroom window to his death. This defendant committed suicide rather than face the prospect of a conviction. Because of the suicide, the case was featured in the media, but the judge's wrongful coercive tactics got little mention.[79]

It is also wrong when a judge uses an excessively high bail amount to persuade a defendant to take a plea. The main purpose of bail is to make sure the defendant shows up in court. However, judges may go along with a prosecutor's vindictive bail request or set very high bail in misdemeanor cases on their own so that the defendant will not be able to make bail. Typically, such judges then tell the defendant that if they plead guilty, they can receive a sentence of "time served" or "no jail time."[79] Such judges routinely fail to advise the defendant of all the repercussions of pleading guilty to a crime that might have led the defendant to decline a plea deal. For example, a guilty plea may greatly increase the likelihood that civil damages might be awarded, or that the defendant might lose other rights, such as forgoing the right to an appeal.[80] Yet given the threat of going to prison, even innocent defendants frequently enter pleas. Consequently, they are branded as convicted criminals, and they must wear that badge of shame for the rest of their lives.

---

[80] Richard Klein, "Judicial Misbehavior in Criminal Cases: It's Not Just the Counsel Who May Be Ineffective and Unprofessional," *Ohio State Journal of Criminal Law*, Vol 4: 195, 2006.

Motivations for Judicial Bias

Political and Prosecutorial Bias

Whether elected or appointed, a judge is beholden to the community and the power brokers that represent the community. In the event the judge is elected, it is common for their nomination to arise from such power brokers — who are apt to choose whomever best represents their interests. Since most community members know little more about the judicial candidates beyond what is revealed in their campaign pictures and a short caption or bio, they can be easily swayed in support of a judicial candidate. And the main influence in these elections is the powers that be. Thus, the main reasons that citizens have little control over what judges do are the following:

❖ The idea that the voters themselves select their judges is something of a farce. The real electors are a few political leaders who do the nominating... Political leaders nominate practically anybody whom they choose. The voters, as a whole, know little more about the candidates than what their campaign pictures may reveal.

❖ That most state judges are elected in near anonymity by voters who do not know who they are compounds the corrupting nature of the campaign process that ensures their lack of impartiality. Thus, the circumstances under which state judges are elected or nominated and confirmed creates a situation in which the people who become state and federal judges serve their own interests and the interests of those to whom they are responsible and not those of society at large.[81]

Under the circumstances, some judges are more apt to seek to serve the interests of themselves and their supporters before that of the general community, as Sherrer explains in the following observations about politics:

- ❖ "Contrary to their carefully cultivated public image of being independent and above the frays of everyday life, judges are influenced and even controlled by powerful and largely-hidden political, financial, personal, and ideological considerations..."[81]

- ❖ "This political influence on judges operates on all levels of the system — from federal to state judgeships, whether elected, appointed, or running unopposed."[81]

The political nature of judges that affects their conduct and rulings occurs because every judge in the United States, whether nominated or elected on the state or federal level, is a product of the political process, just like every other political official...[82]

Similarly, judges tend to display prosecutorial bias, due to both politics and because the sentiments of the surrounding community are usually aligned with the goal of

---

[81] Hans Sherrer in "The Complicity of Judges in the Generation of Wrongful Convictions," *Northern Kentucky Law Review*, Vol. 30:4j.

[82] Hans Sherrer in "The Complicity of Judges in the Generation of Wrongful Convictions," *Northern Kentucky Law Review*, Vol. 30:4j.

the prosecutor to win, and thereby preserve law and order. As Sherrer puts it, judges "have a strong tendency to go with the flow of outside pressures," especially when there is a "media and politically inspired hysteria" campaign to get tough.[82]

This bias toward the prosecution is even more pronounced when a judge has some sort of a personal connection with the prosecutor, such as when a prosecutor had clerked in the judge's office. In any other profession, this would be considered a conflict of interest.

Personal Bias and Discrimination

Ideally, judges should not exhibit a bias or prejudice against any class of people — including prejudice based on race, sex, religion, national origin, disability, age, sexual orientation, or socioeconomic status. But in reality, judges have their own personal biases, leading them to engage in their own form of personal discrimination or judgment.

Judicial history has shown that judges sometimes make biased statements during trials. In one such case, the presiding judge sentenced the female teacher convicted of a sexual relationship with a thirteen-year-old boy to probation instead of the three-year jail sentence to which she had already agreed! He went on to downplay any harm this woman had caused her victim, stating in part: "Maybe it was a way of (the victim), once this did happen, to satisfy his sexual needs. At 13, if you think back, people mature at different ages." The judge then went on to cite newspaper and TV reports in which nine-year-olds were reported to have had sex.[83]

---

[83]Cynthia Gray, "The Line between Legal Error and Judicial Misbehavior: Balancing Judicial Independence and Accountability," *Hofstra Final*, November 24, 2004.

Ultimately, the New Jersey Supreme Court committee found that this judge's statements expressed stereotypical views about the sexual nature of young boys, and noted this judge's views were "...problematic and suspect... fundamentally inconsistent with the meaning and policy of the law that criminalizes the sexual activities between an adult and a minor, boy or girl." Most importantly, the committee complained that the judge was not only mistaken about the law of sexual assault regarding a minor boy, but his remarks reflected a bias against females, and showed a lack of impartiality and open-mindedness in applying the law.[83]

For acting in this manner, the New Jersey judge was publicly reprimanded by the Supreme Court of New Jersey, but was subject to no other penalty, although he might more appropriately have been suspended for a time or permanently.

Unaccountability in a Conveyor Belt System

As has been the case with prosecutors, as discussed in the previous chapter, judges are commonly unaccountable or immune for their actions, no matter how biased they may be in favor of the prosecution. In turn, these biases may result in high economic costs, due to unjust incarcerations or longer sentences than warranted. Moreover, as discussed, these incarcerations mean more costs for each inmate unjustly imprisoned, as well as lost income and family disruptions, resulting in even more costs. In addition, the taxpayer often is on the hook for any governmental assistance the family then qualifies for.

These extra costs are one of the unintended consequences of the impetus judges have to process cases as quickly as possible, so that the system isn't overwhelmed by the sheer numbers of cases that enter it. Instead, to handle the case load, the system is designed like a conveyor belt, with judges having a prime goal of keeping the "assembly-line of the law enforcement system humming smoothly along." Furthermore: "The huge numbers of innocent men and women who are thrown on the conveyor belt and crushed as the gears grind away are treated as if they are unknown, faceless, and their sole value as a human being is being used as fuel to keep the 'law enforcement' machine running."[84]

The Protections of Judges

The result of these pressures to process a huge number of cases quickly, like a justice factory, is a system of unaccountability, with judges protected in numerous ways.

First and most importantly, judges have an absolute immunity to being sued by anyone for anything they do when they are acting in their official capacity. This immunity applies even when a judge is accused of "acting maliciously and corruptly." The rationale for this protection is to enable judges to independently exercise their judicial role without fear of the consequences.[85] As a result, an innocent victim of a judge's intentional and malicious actions cannot sue a judge civilly for the harm the judge has caused. To quote Sherrer: "There is simply no cost to a judge for presiding over the wrongful conviction of an actually innocent person."[85]

About the worst that can happen to biased judges is they do not get reappointed, or they are voted out of office and retire on a comfortable pension. Actual removal from the

---

[84] Hans Sherrer in "The Complicity of Judges in the Generation of Wrongful Convictions," *Northern Kentucky Law Review*, Vol. 30:4j.

[85] Hans Sherrer in "The Complicity of Judges in the Generation of Wrongful Convictions," *Northern Kentucky Law Review*, Vol. 30:4j.

bench is rare. So this is still another cost to the system -- having poorly performing judges who are earning large salaries – the median average for judges in 2011 was $120,130 per year, again varying by state.[86]

Given these protections, the number of poorly performing judges is likely to be quite large, as reflected in an extensive study of judicial misbehavior complaints. This was filed with the judicial conduct commissions in fifty states, according to lawyer Cynthia Gray, director of the American Judicature Society's Center for Judicial Ethics. As she noted, 90% of such complaints are dismissed every year.[87] A key reason for this is that it is considered "unfair to sanction a judge for not being infallible while making hundreds of decisions often under pressure."[87]

In the event a judge is subject to some kind of discipline, rarely is the judge removed from his or her position. Rather, the judge may be reprimanded, censured, or suspended for a time before he or she can return to the bench.

Peers on Judicial Disciplinary Panels

The number of judges that behave poorly in all types of courts — from federal to state courts at various levels — is large, as is the percentage of judges who get away with misbehavior or abuse. A key reason judges usually escape censure is that any disciplinary or investigative panels are usually composed of judges, and such peers are not likely to pass harsh judgment on their fellows.

---

[86] Forrest Time, "Annual Salary for Judges," http://work.chron.com/annual-salary-judges-9479.html

[87] Cynthia Gray, "The Line between Legal Error and Judicial Misbehavior: Balancing Judicial Independence and Accountability," *Hofstra Final*, November 24, 2004.

For example, although 1,163 complaints were filed against federal judges in a one-year period, only four led to any type of disciplinary action, including one public censure.[88] The results were much the same in state courts. Of 909 judicial complaints in California, for instance, only thirty-four or 3.8% resulted in disciplinary actions, ranging from advisory letters to removal from the bench. Of 1,923 complaints in New York, only 3% led to any discipline, including thirty-three letters of caution and twenty-six formal charges.[88]

Given a lack of judicial punishment except in rare cases, it is no wonder judges feel free to behave badly or unethically. Then, too, judges might find it easier to engage in such poor behavior, because their judicial immunity protects them from any civil liability when their actions occur while performing judicial duties. Thus, they can't be held personally accountable, and citizen taxpayers foot the bill for the results of their bad behavior. Just imagine if such a poor performer was discovered in a corporation. He or she would soon be fired, and if fired for cause, would not be eligible for the kind of golden parachute that many corporate leaders have established for themselves. Rather, the corporate poor-performer would quickly be shown the door, and the corporation would not have to pay for the miscreant's continued malfeasance.

---

[88] Gary Hunter and Alex Friedmann, Prison Legal News, June 26, 2012, https://www.prisonlegalnews.org/(S(xsnmk4qmegola055ovintkns))/displayArticle.aspx?artic leid=21570

Limitations on Citizen Complaints

Unfortunately, there are guidelines or rules of operating procedure which exempt most judicial conduct from citizen complaints. One major limitation is that a defendant or any other interested party cannot complain about the actual decision itself — even if it was incorrect. About 90% of all citizen complaints get tossed out on this basis alone.

Citizens can only complain about the judicial process, such as if a judge seemed to have a conflict of interest, or was not paying attention and as a result may have missed crucial evidence in a case. Regrettably, there are only a few ways a defendant can currently seek redress, and many limitations exist here too.

To remedy a verdict, for instance, a person must appeal the ruling. However, while anyone can file an appeal, the appeal is a very complicated process that involves arguing the errors made by the judge and drawing on the relevant points of law in front of a judge. Although the judge handling the appeal is normally a different judge,[89] it is difficult to find an attorney with a specialty in appellate work. Moreover, any appeal is expensive, and most defendants of limited means lack the resources to appeal a case.

Thus, realistically, the only way to try to remedy a judge's bad behavior is to file a complaint against that judge. However, even such a complaint won't normally remedy a bad decision, since as previously noted, about 90% of these complaints are quickly tossed out.

---

[89] The reason for requiring a different judge is so the appellant is not put in the position of appealing the verdict to the very judge who administered the verdict being appealed.

Suggested Solutions

The following solutions are proposed to address the limitations placed on judges and redress the problems of misbehavior by judges:

➢ One area where limitations should be loosened is in the length of a sentence a judge can impose. This restriction is important because, partly due to public pressure, the U.S. imposes longer sentences for most crimes than other countries, and these sentences are many times longer than our northern neighbor Canada imposes. A reason for these unnecessarily long sentences is that mandatory minimum sentences and three strikes laws directed at habitual offenders tie the hands of judges when imposing sentences. But, as state legislators are increasingly beginning to realize, such excessive sentences result in our bloated prison system. However, legislators have the power to call a halt to this trend by rolling back such sentencing laws and guidelines, and the legislators in many conservative states are beginning to do so just that. They are restricting these excessive penalties, and saving their state coffers untold millions with the stroke of a pen -- or in this case, a computer keyboard -- to write new rules.

➢ To redress misbehavior, the major sources of judicial misbehavior should be identified and then guidelines should be established to prevent judges from engaging in such actions. While there is currently little effective recourse to punish judicial misbehavior, the following suggestions are ways we might begin to change the judicial system to reduce such misbehavior, and thereby make the system more cost effective.

➢ Judges should be required to disqualify themselves from any cases that involve attorneys who have clerked with them. Furthermore, a list that shows the names of everyone who has ever clerked for them should be on file with the courts and available for public viewing.

➢ Prospective judges should be required to submit to a psychological assessment to determine if they possess the appropriate judicial temperament and skills. This assessment can be done confidentially and only viewed by a panel certifying the fitness of judges to be appointed or run for office.

➢ Separate elections of judges should be held for inner cities, suburban areas, and rural areas. This change in the voting system would result in returning the exercise of justice back to local populations, which is important because prosecutors and judges are usually elected at the county level. Today, counties that include major cities have a much higher percentage of suburban voters than in the past. This means suburban voters, rarely severely affected by crime, exercise more power over urban criminal justice than in the past, as William J. Stuntz points out in *The Collapse of Criminal Justice*.[90] By instituting separate elections,

---

[90] William J. Stuntz, *The Collapse of American Criminal Justice*, The Belknap Press of Harvard University Press, 2011, p. 7.

judges will be more likely to come from and be responsive to the citizens they represent.

➢ Judicial campaigns should be funded exclusively by public financing in order to prevent big campaign contributions from special interests, which can influence judicial decisions in the future.

➢ Review boards for judicial misconduct should be composed of lawyers from different districts or civilians, with only a minority representation by other judges. A review board that adds lawyers and civilians to it can provide a broader cross-section of the community, and thus it offers a more neutral and objective environment for fairly evaluating a judge's performance.

➢ The judicial disciplinary review process should be transparent, so citizens can see what complaints are being handled and how.

➢ Video cameras should be permitted in the courtroom, but the videos should not be released to the public or the media. Rather, the release of these recordings should be restricted to lawyers in order to document judicial misbehavior as the basis for filing an appeal. In order to keep the recordings from the media, the recordings should be made exempt from the Freedom of Information Act.

➢ Judge Judy-type television shows, which typically show judges behaving badly, should include an advisory that the show is presented purely as entertainment, and does not portray accurately how judges are supposed to comport themselves in a courtroom. This advisory will help to preserve respect for the judiciary at the same time that other guidelines are added to prevent or penalize judicial misconduct.

CHAPTER 6: THE MEDIA MAKE MATTERS WORSE

Today, the media have become complicit in producing unfair treatment, trials, and verdicts for defendants. They sensationalize cases, pick and choose whatever elements of a case make it unusual and "newsworthy," and otherwise draw what often becomes negative public attention to private citizens. Given the ability of the media to pick up local reports and turn them into compelling national stories, even juicy day-to-day gossip can become a national event.

How Cases that Involve Celebrities or Government Officials Can Fare Even Worse

A key reason for prosecutorial bias in the media is that prosecutors are eager to feed the media information. In contrast, defense lawyers generally want to avoid getting their client in the news as much as possible, except where a defendant is so sympathetic that a supportive audience can put pressure on the judge to respond to community sentiment. Consequently, with a few exceptions, in most cases, the media tends to portray defendants as more likely to be guilty than innocent.

For example, the media often repeats statements made about the defendant that have yet to be proven true. Unfortunately, even if these claims later prove erroneous, the damage cannot be undone. While the media seeks to justify its actions in the name of the "public's right to know," it often steps over the line in compromising the defendant's right to a fair trial. Unfortunately, the media generally takes no responsibility for the harm it causes, since after the excitement of the case is over, it is already on to the next "big" story. This kind of harm can occur whether the media supports a sympathetic defendant who is guilty or villainizes a seemingly guilty defendant who is innocent. From the media perspective, it doesn't really matter whether the outcome is justified. What matters to the media is whether it has presented a good story, increased the readership or eyeballs for its story, and thus increased the advertising and financial benefits for the media outlet or publication.

How Media Abuses Make a Defendant Look Guilty

Sometimes, the media can turn public opinion against a defendant just by what they report -- or fail to report -- about statements made in public, interviews with the press, or in court. As such, the media can make an innocent defendant appear remarkably guilty by bringing up past unsavory behaviors or associations, suggesting a motive, or otherwise framing various past circumstances to support a theory that purportedly "proves" a predisposition to commit a crime.

While judges generally do not allow such prejudicial examples to be presented in the actual criminal case, they are generally unable to prevent the media from reporting such information outside the courtroom under the guise of "investigative journalism." Unfortunately, potential jurors are then commonly exposed to such information, despite jury instructions to disregard outside-of-the-courtroom accounts, and that information can influence their supposedly neutral analysis of the evidence and testimony in a case. As such, sometimes defense lawyers ask to have a case moved to another location, one that has not reported too much on the story.

The media can also make a defendant seem guilty by playing up the defendant's reaction after being charged with a crime. If the individual's reaction seems lighthearted or inappropriate, the media may target that behavior as a sign of guilt — something which can also influence jurors. This was the case in the Casey Anthony trial, in which Casey was charged with drowning her young child in a backyard pool.[91] Though she was later found not guilty due to conflicting evidence in a lurid trial that presented her as a party girl rather than a caring mom who found her daughter in the pool, she was never able to escape the portrayal in the media where she was sometimes dubbed "the most hated woman in the world." So she was reduced to living as a virtual hermit for several years, ever seeking to evade the eye of the media, eager to find more examples of her terrible behavior as proof of her real guilt.

---

[91] John Cloud, "How the Casey Anthony Murder Case Became the Social-Media Trial of the Century," *Time Magazine*, June 16, 2011
http://content.time.com/time/nation/article/0,8599,2077969,00.html

Despite such biased stories, one way the media protects itself from being accused of bias against a defendant is by claiming that it is "just a messenger" and merely reporting on what was already "said by the police or prosecutors." However, the media has great leeway in what it reports as that messenger, so it can selectively pick out information that supports its bias in a particular case to make a defendant seem more guilty or innocent. To some extent, the media may draw on what appears to already be popular opinion about whether the defendant did something or not. In other cases, the media's position can help to create or shape the popular view.

In addition, the media commonly releases information on TV or the Internet with insertions of numerous "alleged" descriptors to suggest that the defendant is only a "possible" suspect who has "allegedly" committed a crime. The media's use of the word "alleged" protects it from defamation -- either written libel or spoken slander, although the use of the term "alleged" has the effect of suggesting that the person actually did what he or she is "alleged" to have done. Just listen to the morning or nightly news, and you will hear the word "alleged" used numerous times in a daily report on national or local crime. Often listeners and viewers disregard the use of the term "alleged" and consider that the person is likely the perpetrator; else why would he or she be considered a likely suspect.

This reaction occurs, because nearly invariably, even when the defendant's guilt is qualified by the term "alleged," the public responds with an assumption of the defendant's guilt. "Innocent until proven guilty" becomes "guilty until proven innocent," and it becomes difficult to change people's minds after the fact, even if ultimately they are shown a more plausible interpretation of the facts.

Psychological research has shown that once people take a position, they are more receptive to information in the future that confirms the impression they have already formed than to listening to and/or accepting information that contradicts their position. As Chief Justice Thurgood Marshall has pointed out, a juror "will listen more with favor to that testimony which confirms than to that which will change his opinion; it is not to be expected that he will weigh evidence or argument as fairly as a man whose judgment is not made up in the case."[92]

Notorious Pre-Trial (and Trial) Publicity

The big problem with too much publicity for a case is that it not only attracts viewers and sells newspapers or draws viewers to websites, but it can destroy a defendant's chance to get a fair trial. That is what happened in the notorious Sam Sheppard trial in which the defendant, a doctor, was accused of murdering his wife. In this 1954 case, Sheppard maintained an intruder knocked him unconscious and killed his wife, but the coroner (Sam Gerber) was overheard telling a detective, "It's obvious that the doctor did it," a quote that soon appeared in the media.

The press turned against Sheppard with a fury before he was even charged with anything! Statements and leaks by the prosecution helped add fuel to the media fire, with the Cleveland Press quoting Assistant Prosecutor John Mahon as declaring four days after the murder: "In my twenty-three years of criminal investigation, I have never seen such

---

[92] Jaime N. Morris: "The Anonymous Accused: Protecting Defendants' Rights in High-Profile Criminal Cases," 44 B.C.L. Rv 901 (2003), http:/lawdigitalcommons.bc.edu/bclr/vol44/iss3/6.

flagrant stalling as in this case by the family." Soon thereafter, a front-page editorial screamed out to law enforcement and the public with the cry, "WHY NO INQUEST? DO IT NOW, DR. GERBER."[93]

The police quickly responded with Sheppard's arrest. By the time the actual trial started, it had already become a media circus: "Celebrity journalists flocked to the city for a trial that promised sex, mystery, and intrigue in abundance."[94] Amazingly, even the judge — Judge Edward Blythin — shared his opinion of Sheppard's guilt in the ongoing case with a reporter, although the reporter only reported his statements nearly a decade later, after the judge's death. Apparently, the judge told the reporter: "The case is open and shut... he's guilty as hell."

Despite defense motions to move the trial out of the city in which the murder occurred, or at least delay it until publicity about the case died down, the judge refused. So the trial proceeded with a jury already mired in public opinion against Sheppard. Worse, the jury's ability to remain impartial was further compromised when Cleveland newspapers published all of the jurors' photos and names. Given the strong community sentiment against Sheppard, what identified juror would dare buck community opinion and approach the case without bias?

Not surprisingly, the jury found Sheppard guilty of second-degree murder, and Judge Blythin sentenced him to life in prison. However, things turned around when a new defense lawyer, F. Lee Bailey, took over the case after the death of Sheppard's first lawyer. In 1963, Bailey filed a

---

[93] Douglas O. Linder, *The Dr. Sam Sheppard Trial*, 2006; http://law2.umkc.edu/faculty/projects/ftrials/sheppard/sheppardaccount.html
[94] Douglas O. Linder, *The Dr. Sam Sheppard Trial*, 2006; http://law2.umkc.edu/faculty/projects/ftrials/sheppard/sheppardaccount.html

petition that claimed, "Prejudicial publicity before and during the 1954 trial violated Sheppard's right to the due process of law."[94] Eventually, the case reached the U.S. Supreme Court, which agreed that the publicity surrounding Sheppard's trial had prejudiced his "right to trial by an impartial jury." The Court also provided some guidelines to help judges keep the courtroom impartial in the face of publicity from the media. In particular, the Court said a judge should:

- ❖ Set rules for in-court conduct by reporters;
- ❖ Grant continuances for a later trial if the trial might be influenced by a high level of media publicity;
- ❖ Grant a change of venue to keep prospective jurors unbiased;
- ❖ Admonish the jury to ignore publicity;
- ❖ Sequester the jury to insulate them from publicity; and/or
- ❖ Issue protective gag orders prohibiting out of court statements by trial participants.[95]

However, the Court's ruling did not take Sheppard off the hook, because within days prosecutors decided to retry him. This time, though, the defense prevailed by bringing up blood-spatter evidence that showed the killer was left-handed, whereas Sheppard was right-handed. F. Lee Bailey also showed there was blood on the closet door that came from neither Sheppard nor his wife, and was presumably left by the killer. As a result, the jury acquitted Sheppard.[96] Yet, despite his acquittal, Sheppard remained guilty or at least damaged

---

[95] "Chapter Seven: Press and Fair Trial," www.radford.edu/wkovarik/class/law/1.7fairtrial.htm
[96] *The Sam Sheppard Murder Case,* About.com Guide, About.com Crime/Punishment, crime.about.com/od/history/p/sheppard_sam.htm.

goods in the eyes of the public, and he was never able to return to his practice as before. In fact, he died an early death as a broken man, showing the enduring damage that a trial by media can do when the defendant is judged guilty in the court of public opinion.

Thus, in Sheppard's case, even an eventual acquittal didn't mean Sheppard was truly free, because the media played a critical role in distorting the justice process from the very beginning. That's why the U.S Supreme Court recognized that the negative publicity had made it impossible for Sheppard to get a fair trial, and he certainly was never able to return to the life that had been so unfairly ripped from him.

To temper down such abuses, in tabloid-crazed Britain, newspapers, periodicals, and broadcasters can only publish or include some basic factual information about a case in their reports: the identity of the court and the name of the judge; the names, ages, home addresses and occupations of the accused and witnesses; the offense or offenses charged; the names of the lawyers in the proceeding; any date and place to which the proceedings are adjourned; any arrangements for bail; and whether legal aid was granted to the accused. This approach is designed to keep the reporters from reporting details of the case that may prove inflammatory to the defendant.[97] Yet, in practice, the British press suffers from some of the same serious breaches of privacy for defendants, such as headlines splashed across a tabloid hinting at the alleged wrongs of the defendant. The British public that

---

[97] Judicial Studies Board, "Reporting Restrictions in the Crown Court," http://www.societyofeditors.co.uk/userfiles/file/Reporting Restrictions Crown Court.pdf

follows the tabloids laps up these hints of scandalous crimes as if the guilty verdict is all but determined in advance.

Across Multiple Platforms and from Unnamed Sources

These aforementioned cases are just the tip of the iceberg, since the media can turn virtually any case into a highly publicized one—and more so in today's world by virtue of the multiple media platforms now in existence. Nowadays, many mediums, including online e-zines, news aggregators like the conservative *Drudge Report* and liberal *Huffington Post*, individual bloggers, social media commentators on Facebook, Twitter, and Google+, and media on mobile devices, are apt to pick up on a story released initially by one outlet, sometimes without confirming the information. Plus now there are all sorts of independent news posters on quickly created websites and Facebook pages that sensationalize the news to support a particular political point of view.

Given all of these outlets, once a story gets promoted on one of these news outlets, it can quickly go viral, whether true or not. A recent example is a story about an alleged University of Virginia rape case reported by *Rolling Stone* magazine in 2014 and then picked up by the national media. It caused tremendous turmoil for both the school and those accused, though it was soon found to be a false allegation.[98]

At one time, the courtroom operated fairly free of the influence of newspapers, since news articles relevant to the case at hand were cut out of the daily paper before it was

---

[98] http://www.washingtonpost.com/blogs/erik-wemple/wp/2015/01/22/e-mails-reflect-massive-impact-of-discredited-rolling-stone-story-on-u-va

handed to the jurors. But today, it is difficult to redact anything, given the pervasiveness of the news on multiple media platforms. Many jurors are liable to become aware of and be influenced by information through simply reading the news of the day on the Internet, or reading through their emails, which can include updates and flashes from various news sources.

Moreover, some jurors, already accustomed to tweeting or blogging about whatever they are doing in their personal lives, may find it easy to slip and make an inappropriate comment about their participation in a trial.

Oftentimes, too, a reporter will cite an unnamed "source" as the basis for a story, and claim it is a "journalist's privilege" to protect the identity of the source.

Racial Bias

Racial bias, expressed by the media, is another contributor to increased tension between the races that sometimes spills into destructive riots, leads to crimes against individuals based on race, and in multiple ways increases economic and social costs. In addition, the tension can contribute to a climate of fear, making a community less desirable as a place to live. Here are some of the many ways that racial bias contributes to these costs.

Often, the race of a defendant or victim plays a part in contributing to the public's belief, inflamed by the media, that a defendant is guilty. The result can be not only that an innocent person gets wrongly put away, but the real killer walks free, and in many cases returns to a life of crime, resulting in more social and economic costs.

A good example of how racial bias can poison the atmosphere surrounding a case is the highly publicized

Rodney King case, where a predominantly white jury exonerated white L.A. police officers who brutally beat King. This outcome provoked a riot, which cost 1.3 billion dollars for business and for the city itself.[99],[100]

Racial overtones likewise contributed to the 1995 O.J. Simpson case, which cost the city of Los Angeles millions in direct court costs plus extra police on duty to keep the peace on the streets outside the courthouse. This beefed-up police presence was needed, because the trial had become a true media circus, with hundreds of vans, reporters, photographers, and cameramen camped outside to report on the latest news for the day.[101]

Early on, a racial divide surfaced in how whites and blacks viewed the case, which turned into a litmus test of race relations. Based on Simpson's behavior in the SUV "chase" that dragged on for hours on live TV, most whites assumed he had to be guilty. The case turned on the exposure of racist attitudes by police detective Mark Fuhrman and defense attorney Johnnie Cochran's pithy saying: "If the gloves don't fit, you must acquit." Whites formed the impression that O.J. was guilty, but escaped true justice because of his celebrity status and team of slick, expensive lawyers. By contrast, African-Americans commonly thought O.J. had been railroaded by the system because of his race and marriage to a white woman.

While Simpson was eventually declared "not guilty" by a predominantly African-American jury in the criminal case, he was found guilty by a primarily white jury in a subsequent civil case. Later, he was sent to prison for leading

[99]http://content.time.com/time/specials/2007/la_riot/article/0,28804,1614117_16 14084_16148 31,00.html

[100] http://www.chicagotribune.com/chi-insurance-civil-unrest-riots-bix-gfx-20141126-htmlstory.html

[101] http://www.famous-trials.com/simpson/1862-home

a group of associates into a hotel room to rob a man selling his sports paraphernalia, because he believed the items had been stolen from him in the first place. For someone with no prior criminal record, he received an especially stiff sentence -- a minimum of seven years in prison -- since one of his associates had pulled out a gun. Commonly, this verdict was viewed as payback for the acquittal in the criminal trial, since the general public was widely convinced of his guilt.

In the past year, several new OJ portrayals appeared on television, one of which involved several episodes on CNN. It won several awards because it dealt not only with OJ and his case, but it also highlighted the pronounced division between blacks and whites over his guilt or innocence and exoneration as a murderer. It pointed out how blacks feel victimized by the system and consider it a victory if any black is exonerated.

Even OJ's recent parole hearing became a subject of controversy, influenced by the racial divide, with whites generally hoping he would remain in prison, while blacks felt he should be freed, since he was unjustly imprisoned in the first place. Ultimately, he was paroled at the age of 70, but he remains a pariah, shunned by whites, who still see him as guilty and a very tarnished former celebrity star. Stay tuned for more media attention when he is released.

In turn, this continued hostility of blacks towards the system, based on the perception that it unfairly victimizes them, has contributed to continued costly resistance. A recent example of this is the spread of the Black Lives Matter movement, which has fanned the flames, especially in the inner cities, resulting in protests, some of which have turned violent or resulted in looting. So aside from any concerns about injustice, these encounters are reflected in increasing economic costs and an environment which is less safe. A big fear is that violence might spill over from the inner cities to company offices and to residences in the suburbs.

The Trayvon Martin/George Zimmerman case in Florida is another good example of how racial tension can lead to violence and more economic costs. The case initially began as a killing by a local neighborhood-watch captain who thought a man he saw in a gated community was acting suspiciously. At first the man tried to run; then Zimmerman caught up and they tussled; and Zimmerman fired, killing Martin. Zimmerman claimed he had fired in fear of his life, thinking Martin was about to grab his gun.

However, Martin was African-American, while Zimmerman was perceived as white, though he is part Hispanic. As a consequence, Zimmerman was quickly blamed as the bad guy who used racial profiling to first stop Martin and then to kill him. As a result, the killing easily fit into a portrayal of whites who use racial profiling to target African-Americans as criminals. Soon, African-American leaders were calling attention to the case, and the national media then picked up the story, portraying Martin as an African-American martyr who was killed because Zimmerman picked on him due to racial profiling. Public perception quickly gelled to view Zimmerman as a prejudiced racial profiler who had targeted an innocent victim walking through the community because of his skin color. Only later did media images surface of Zimmerman with wounds he previously claimed he received from Martin, and Zimmerman eventually was acquitted.[102] However, he was never able to return to his former role in the community; instead, his image was forever tarnished as a racist. Some subsequent relatively minor

---

[102] http://www.nytimes.com/2013/07/14/us/george-zimmerman-verdict-trayvon-martin.html?_r=0

incidents were played up to create a negative perception of him in the public eye, such as when he had a fight with a girlfriend or was stopped for a DUI.

More recent incidents have occurred with the death of Michael Brown in Ferguson, Missouri,[103] and Eric Garner in New York City,[104] at the hands of the police. Both cases garnered significant attention by the national media. The popular press tended to present these cases as unjustified police killings which were unnecessary, since Brown seemed to be running away from the police when shot, while Garner was struggling for breath while the police were trying to restrain him. But in both cases, the grand juries decided not to indict the police responsible for the killings. Both decisions sparked large protests in response to the popular perception that the police were guilty and that a jury had unfairly exonerated the police of any guilt.

Afterwards, the media largely continued to support this anti-police point of view. Later, when information came out supporting Wilson's claim that he had defended himself against an attack by Brown, and witnesses had lied trying to support Brown's case, the mainstream media largely downplayed this information. Consequently, the truth of what really happened got limited exposure. It would seem the media was already invested in supporting the story of police violence and racial profiling against African-Americans, which had first led to the spreading protests. So in this initial Ferguson case, it would seem the media played into a political agenda to demonize the police and build on the fury against profiling sparked by the Trayvon Martin case. Then, those

---

[103] http://www.nytimes.com/interactive/2014/08/13/us/ferguson-missouri-town-under-siege-after-police-shooting.html?_r=0
[104] http://www.nydailynews.com/new-york/nypd-eric-garner-chokehold-death-not-indicted-article-1.2031841

media accounts helped to fuel the spreading outrage that continued to increase racial tensions and could even lead to further tension.

Though the media could play a more positive force to use the power of the press to tamp down tensions by showing examples of different racial groups working together in peace and harmony in different arenas, it does not do so. Why not? Most likely it's because stories of violence are what sells newspapers and glues viewers to the news on their television sets, the Internet, or iPhones. As a result, since violence is a more dramatic and therefore represents a more interesting story to draw readers and viewers, that's what the media tend to emphasize. Even more recent incidents in Baltimore and Cleveland have played out similarly.

The liberal racial bias seems to target whites. In all these cases, the mostly liberal media not only contributed to the portrayal of defendants as guilty before the trials even began, but they also played a role in inflaming race relations. In turn, as previously pointed out, such conflicts tend to spill into violence, which can lead to death, property damage, and other crimes associated with urban upheavals, including looting and arson. And of course, such events increase the costs of policing, handling these cases in the courts, the high costs of corrections, and the loss of the productivity of those who end up being incarcerated due to the spiral of violence triggered by racial conflict.

Stereotyping

Stereotyping occurs all the time in crime news reporting. A pro-prosecution slant arises since local and wire service reporters have long-established relationships with law-enforcement agencies and prosecutors who "serve superiors with strong career incentives to maximize publicity for crime-fighting successes."[105] Therefore, as Entman and Gross point out, reporters engage in an overreliance on public officials, overuse of standardized story scripts and familiar stereotypes, and 'pack journalism' — the tendency of reporters from nominally competitive news organizations to converge on the same subjects in a feeding frenzy. In the case of crime coverage, these media routines can facilitate a pro-prosecution slant that appears across news coverage, when law-enforcement officials are eager to promote claims of guilt. This use of stereotyping can be especially damaging for African-Americans and Latinos.[106]

Criminal Profiling

While racial profiling has been rightly accused of wrongly targeting suspects based on their racial or ethnic characteristics, criminal profiling is equally dangerous. Take the case of Richard Jewell, originally considered a hero for discovering a pipe bomb planted in a knapsack at the Centennial Olympic Park in Atlanta during the 1996 Summer Olympics. Jewell was working as a security guard, when he discovered the bomb on park grounds, alerted the police, and helped evacuate people from the area before the bomb exploded, saving hundreds of people from death or injury.

---

[105] "Race to Judgment: Stereotyping Media and Criminal Defendants," *Law and Contemporary Problems*, Vol. 71:93, 2008, Robert M. Entman and Kimberly Gross pp. 95-103, 128.
[106] "Race to Judgment: Stereotyping Media and Criminal Defendants," *Law and Contemporary Problems*, Vol. 71:93, 2008, Robert M. Entman and Kimberly Gross pp. 95-103, 128.

Initially, the press feted Jewell as a hero for his discovery and quick thinking that saved many lives.[107]

However, three days after his discovery, Jewell became a suspect, for he fit an FBI "lone bomber" criminal profile. For the next three months after the *Atlanta Journal-Constitution* revealed that the FBI viewed Jewell as a possible suspect due to this profile, Jewell's life became a living hell. Reporters speculated that Jewell was a "failed law enforcement officer who may have planted the bomb so he could find it and be a hero"[108] These reports led two of the bombing victims to file suits against Jewell, who consequently became the target of jokes on late-night TV.

The media and public pressure on Jewell only began to ease up after his attorneys hired an ex-FBI agent to administer a lie-detector test that he passed, and the FBI realized he would have been unable to make a call warning authorities about the bomb.[109]

Consequently, he prevailed in a series of suits against the media, including NBC News and the *New York Post*, for some of their remarks. Eventually, Jewell was completely exonerated when the real bomber, Eric R. Rudolph, pleaded guilty to the attack.[110]

In another notorious case of a press lynching involving some deaths from anthrax mailings, the press carried out attacks not just once, but twice, since after the first defendant proved innocent, they went after another target. Unfortunately, this second individual killed himself, and was only to be shown to most likely be innocent after his death.

---

[107] Kevin Sack, "Richard Jewell, 44, Hero of Atlanta Attack, Dies," *New York Times,* August 30, 2007. http://www.nytimes.com/2007/08/30/us/30jewell.html
[108] "Richard Jewell," Wikipedia, en.wikipedia.org/wiki/Richard Jewell
[109] http://www.columbia.edu/itc/journalism/j6075/edit/readings/jewell.html
[110] "Richard Jewell," Wikipedia, en.wikipedia.org/wiki/Richard Jewell

The case began in September 2001, when envelopes containing spores of anthrax were mailed to several press organizations and two Democratic Senators. The envelopes were accompanied by letters that suggested they had been sent by an Arab extremist, or someone posing as one, since they included the statements, "We have this anthrax... Death to America... Death to Israel." Whoever sent them, the threat was very real, since the letters resulted in 5 deaths and 17 other people becoming ill.[111]

The ensuing media coverage and copycat hoax mailings contributed to a sense of panic among the general population. Meanwhile, the FBI and law enforcement were subjected to increasing pressure to quickly apprehend the killer or killers. It was in this climate of growing fear that the FBI focused on the limited number of American scientists who might have a working knowledge of anthrax. One of these scientists was Steven Hatfill, a medical doctor, who had once worked at the Army's elite Medical Research Institute of Infectious Diseases (USAMRIID), which had stocks of anthrax. Instead of conducting a quiet exploratory investigation, as is common in the early stages of any investigation, the FBI did the opposite in the Hatfill case. A team of agents conducted a search of the doctor's apartment accompanied by TV news cameras broadcasting the search live.

This search precipitated a media offensive in a "war" against Hatfill. Reporters and camera crews swarmed into Hatfill's apartment after he signed a consent form to let the FBI search, as he felt he had nothing to hide.

The fallout from the investigation and media coverage resulted in Hatfill quickly losing his job for a large defense contractor — and no one else wanted to hire him. Attorney

[111]David Freed, "The Wrong Man," *The Atlantic*, May 2010, p. 2.

General John Ashcroft also publicly declared Hatfill to be a "person of interest." Soon afterwards, FBI agents grilled his friends, tapped his phone, and installed surveillance cameras outside his girlfriend's condo, where he had relocated due to his loss of income. As described by David Freed, in an Atlantic article appropriately titled "The Wrong Man"[112]:

"The result was an unrelenting stream of inflammatory innuendo that dominated front pages and television news. Hatfill found himself trapped, the powerless central player in what Connolly (Hatfill's attorney) describes as 'a story about the two most powerful institutions in the United States, the government and the press, ganging up on an innocent man. It's Kafka.'"[113]

Hatfill's own effort to hold a press conference to proclaim his innocence after the searches of his apartment had no effect. There was almost no coverage in the news, and after that he became a virtual recluse who turned to drinking and stopped reading newspapers altogether. Hatfield claims what saved him from suicide was that he began to study old medical textbooks like he was back in school. Once a student again, his dreams of his eventual payday from suing the Justice Department and the reporters and newspapers that defamed him vanished. At that point, he just wanted to help people, and instead visited Sri Lanka to help treat the victims of a huge tsunami.

Meanwhile, despite all the FBI efforts to investigate Hatfill for six years, the agents were unable to provide any firm evidence, and he was never indicted. Consequently, Hatfill initiated a series of lawsuits. The government eventually settled for $5.8 million, and there was an out-of-

---

[112] www.theatlantic.com/magazine/print/2010/05/the-wrong-man/8019
[113] Ibid.

court settlement with both *Vanity Fair* and *The Reader's Digest*.

The only thing that stopped the FBI-press barrage against Hatfill was when new investigators reexamined the evidence in the case in early 2007, at which time agents came to believe that Hatfill never really had access to the anthrax at USAMRIID. Their new target, Bruce Edward Ivins, was a microbiologist who worked at the center and had access to the anthrax virus. The FBI and media proceeded to give Ivins the same relentless treatment as they had given Hatfill. Like Hatfill, Ivins was soon out of his job at a lab where he had worked for twenty-eight years. Meanwhile, the press began looking into "the pathology of Ivins' life" and linked him, although speculatively, to the murders.

Unlike Hatfill, Ivins did not possess the necessary mental stamina to withstand the pressure. Suffering from depression and anxiety, he entered into a voluntary two-week stay at a psychiatric hospital. Two weeks later, he killed himself with an overdose of Tylenol. Even after his death, though, the press did not let up, suggesting Ivins's suicide was proof of his guilt.

As it turns out, Ivins may not have been the real anthrax killer either. In July 2011, the Department of Justice filed court documents claiming that Ivins did not possess the equipment necessary to have conducted the attacks. In short, the FBI, along with the media, targeted not one, but two, innocent victims in the anthrax attacks, and the relentless media coverage helped destroy Stephen Hatfill's career and led Bruce Edwards Ivins to take his life.[114]

Public interest in unsolved cold cases probably fueled interest in the 20th anniversary of Jon Benet Ramsey's death.

---

[114] www.theatlantic.com/magazine/print/2010/05/the-wrong-man/8019

At least three separate revisits by different media organizations were made late last year. One of them, CBS, hired three experts who strongly intimated that Jon Benet's brother Burke was the culprit, even though they made certain to avoid a direct accusation, presumably to avoid defamation charges if they were wrong. Burke then sued CBS.[115] Whether he is guilty or not, Burke's life has basically been ruined in the court of public opinion, and he had no real opportunity to defend himself, other than a plaintive denial to Dr. Phil, which has no legal standing. So a widespread public suspicion of his guilt remains, though it could well be wrong. Thus, however flawed our criminal justice system, the media should not attempt to substitute for it.

Perhaps the worst bias against defendants is that accorded by pundits in the media. According to Entman and Gross, certain opinion columnists and cable television personalities are "far and away the worst offenders in framing from a one-side prosecution perspective." They cite cable talk shows such as The Nancy Grace Show as the "most egregiously imbalanced."[116]

The Growing Problem of Bias and False News

Unfortunately, rather than socially responsible journalism, much of what poses as journalistic writing and news reporting is designed to excite and titillate readers with slanted news and exposés about defendants. Then, once

---

[115] https://www.usatoday.com/story/life/tv/2016/12/28/jonbenet-ramseys-brother-sues-cbs-750m-over-series/95933158/
[116] "Race to Judgment: Stereotyping Media and Criminal Defendants" *Law and Contemporary Problems*, Vol. 71:93, 2008, Robert M. Entman and Kimberly Gross pp. 95-103, 128.

captured by the media headlights, such stories — whether true, false, or exaggerated — can be blasted everywhere.

Regrettably, the accusations of "fake news" uttered from different political points of view have only muddied the media waters. While some of the accusations are right on, revealing blatant lies, distortions, and exaggerations, other charges have simply been against media accounts one doesn't like, even though these are accurate reporting. The problem for the average citizen is not being able to tell the difference, so these conflicting and contradictory accounts often continue to circulate and support a particular position. But for someone who really wants to know the truth, it is difficult to tell what is really true and what isn't.

Thus, journalists need to recognize and take stock of the harm that can be done to defendants and their families, especially ones that eventually prove innocent, when false and biased accounts are spread as the truth. Likewise, broadcasters need to present more balanced news stories and include in-depth stories about criminal justice subjects, so people can better understand the biases woven through the criminal justice system and put pressure on their legislators to correct them.

Yet there are some recent signs of hope. By 2013, a small but growing number of television shows and movies were paying more attention to flaws in the criminal justice system, even if primarily from a liberal perspective. A *Charlie Rose* episode featured a panel discussion on prison reform that involved author Michelle Alexander and filmmaker Eugene Jarecki,[117] and an *Independent Lens* episode on PBS featured a Eugene Jarecki documentary.[118] A

---

[117] http://www.tv.com/shows/charlie-rose/watch/marion-cotillard-andrew-solomon-a-discussion-about-prison-reform-2615132
[118] http://www.pbs.org/independentlens/house-i-live-in/

60 Minutes episode featured the case of Michael Morton, wrongly convicted of his wife's murder and exonerated after twenty-five years in prison.[119,120] In addition, two movies, *West of Memphis*[121] and *Central Park Five*"[122] featured stories of two groups of juveniles — one white and the other black — convicted of serious crimes (murder and rape) which they did not commit.

As African-Americans tend to identify with black victims and black defendants — and whites do the same with white defendants and white victims — there is a real need to more effectively balance the racial composition of juries in racially charged cases. Concurrently, the potentially inflammatory nature of these cases requires the media to act in a more socially conscious fashion. They should take on more responsibility to report such cases with restraint.

In short, the media needs to avoid pouring kerosene on the fire at any point in these — and all other cases involving racial issues — to avoid inflaming these cases any further and contributing to a popular but unjust result. Any unjust convictions place an unneeded burden on the criminal justice system -- from an arrest to a trial to a verdict. Then, the cost of corrections and the loss of the falsely convicted individual from productive work result in more economic losses to society. Thus, the media's goal of making short term financial gains by catering to the public's appetite for dramatic crime stories contributes both to biased unjust verdicts and to unnecessary costs to the criminal justice system.

---

[119] http://www.texasmonthly.com/topics/michael-morton

[120] Michael Morton, *Getting Life: An Innocent Man's 25-Year Journey from Prison to Peace,* Simon & Schuster, 2014.

[121] http://ffilms.org/west-of-memphis-2012

[122] http://www.pbs.org/kenburns/centralparkfive

Suggested Solutions

Given this serious problem of the media sensationalizing and inaccurately reporting on such controversial news stories, here are some ways the media might be called to account. The result will be more responsible, reliable reporting that involves presenting stories based on the facts, rather than promoting sensationalized stories where gossip and innuendo turn innocent victims into criminals without any proof that they are. To this end, the following solutions are suggested:

➢ Names of individuals charged with a crime should not be reported by the media. Reports should mention only that individuals have been apprehended and whether or not they were released on bail. This anonymity should also remain in the case during and after a trial, unless the trial results in a guilty verdict.

➢ The media should not be allowed to report what they learn from prosecutors, unless the defense lawyers are also allowed to comment on that information.

➢ Reporters, publishers, and producers who have produced false stories should be required to do follow-up stories, apart from any other penalties, to make up for any false information and vilification of the subject of the story. The media should do these follow-ups within a certain date of their initial offense in reporting a false story, and this story should be placed on the first page of a newspaper or in the first 3 to 5 minutes of a news story on TV or in the Internet media.

➤ The publishers and owners of the broadcast and Internet media should be held more closely responsible for the stories printed or posted through their platform. For more serious breaches, they should continue to be held liable civilly or criminally, along with reporters, for false or sensationalized stories causing harm to a particular individual or organization. This liability for false and sensationalized stories should be extended when the story leads to widespread protests that cause extensive damages, such as to a community whose neighborhood is trashed due to a protest sparked by a false story.

➤ The standard for a reporter or publication should be changed from reporting what is simply alleged or rumored to reporting what is actually known or making it very clear that there is a lack of actual facts in a case. Reporters should not be allowed to use the term "alleged" to permit the attribution of false and damaging claims to an individual or organization.

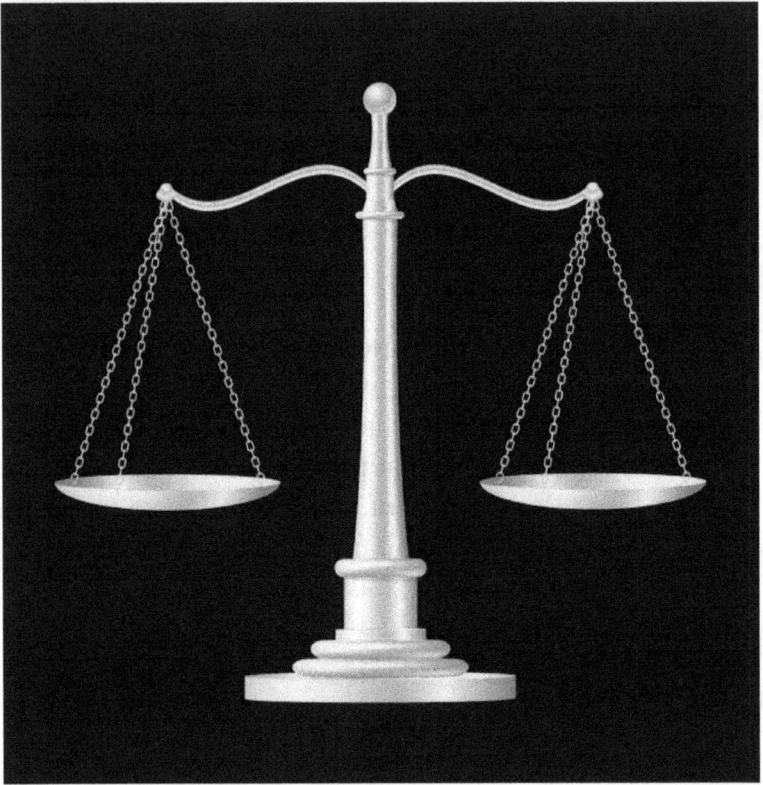

CHAPTER 7: NINE PRESCRIPTIONS TO FIX OUR BROKEN CRIMINAL JUSTICE SYSTEM

How can we fix our broken criminal justice system? One effort to overhaul it goes back almost a decade, if not longer, and the need to fix it has become more urgent than ever.

In March 2009, Senator James Webb issued a call for a national commission to completely overhaul the system -- a commission vitally needed now more than ever. In particular, the commission should find answers to these key questions raised by Senator Webb:

* Why are so many more Americans in prison compared with other countries and with our own history?
* What do our current prison and criminal justice policies cost our nation in lost tax dollars and lost opportunities?
* How can we better change our nation's drug policies?
* How can we better end violence in our prisons and on our city streets?
* How can we more effectively diagnose and treat mental illness, since so many of our prisoners, drug addicts, and homeless individuals are mentally ill?
* How can we create effective re-entry programs, so our communities can assimilate former offenders and encourage them to become productive citizens?

❖ How can we protect ourselves against the growing violence of internationally based gangs, which are spreading through our cities?[123]

Fixes for the System

The following discussion highlights the major problems that require correction and suggested remedies.

---

[123] James Webb http://parade.com/104193/senatorjimwebb/its-time-to-change-the-law/ http://parade.com/104227/senatorjimwebb/why-we-must-fix-our-prisons

Prescription # 1: Better Safeguard our Police and Citizens

The police are our first line of defense in combatting crime. The overwhelming majority of police officers perform their duties selflessly and with devotion. They risk their lives every day, and their families live in constant fear that something will happen to them. They are exposed to very risk-laden situations. In spite of those dangers, surprisingly, most never use their guns or even need to draw them. But as tensions grow once more between the police and black urban communities, they need additional safeguards, and so do the citizens they apprehend.

One of the riskiest situations that police face is the normally minor car stop. Most often these stops are for minor speeding, erratic driving, or expired license plate offenses. Yet these infractions can represent just the tip of the iceberg, providing the basis for discovering much more serious offenses. In such circumstances, the driver of the car and its occupants may be very nervous and operate on a hair trigger, particularly if they have a weapon available. The outcome of these situations is all too frequently deadly, either for the driver, the police or both.

Any incident that results in the fatality of a police officer in the line of duty is a monumental tragedy that should be avoided at all costs. Any incident that results in the fatality of an innocent person represents a failure of law enforcement and most likely leads to a crushing end to the career or finances of the officer involved. Frictions between police and minority communities also need to be reduced. The following should be done to reduce the hazards of these points of police-citizen confrontation -- both to save lives and reduce costs to the criminal justice system.

➢ All police officers on patrol and their vehicles should be equipped with cameras that record all incidents in order to show what really happened.

➢ Police officers should not be required to get out of their vehicle for a routine traffic stop. At night, officers should instruct drivers to turn on their car interior lights and place both hands on the steering wheel.[124] They should record the license plate of the offending vehicle and audibly advise the driver on a broadcast from their car that he or she has been issued an electronic citation which will require an appearance in court on a particular date. If and when technology permits, a photograph of a driver's license held out the driver's side window could be taken, too. These procedures to automate giving a ticket will greatly reduce the risk to police and civilians alike.

➢ Profiling of minorities by police should be greatly restricted to include stops only when: 1) a weapon has been displayed or fired in a local incident in the past hour, and 2) a description of *both* the suspect and a vehicle used in that incident match the vehicle spotted by the police. This requirement to connect the suspect stopped to a clear description of a wanted suspect will reduce the number of friction points between minority communities and the police and may save many innocent lives.

➢ Profiling minorities who are on foot in the close vicinity of a crime should be restricted to one hour

---

[124] Frank Fellone, "For Night Stops, Light Up Interior," *Arkansas Democrat-Gazette*, September 16, 2017.

following the crime. This will limit any targeting of suspects to those who can realistically be close enough to actually have committed the crime in that time frame. In the event a suspect is observed within this area in this limited time-period, two officers must be involved in any stop and frisk apprehension. If the suspect runs, the police may follow but should not shoot to kill, unless the suspect appears to be reaching for a weapon, in which case a police officer would be justified in shooting in self-defense.

➤ The use of deadly force guidelines and the training for applying them need to be overhauled and standardized for those situations which present a clear and present danger for police officers. Currently the use of force guidelines vary widely by locality, and so does police training. While such training may be impractical for small rural police forces, their officers should be required to receive such training at the nearest larger police force facility.

Prescription # 2: Reform the Bail Reform Act

One of the most devastating things about being arrested for low income individuals is a lack of ability to afford bail. Many innocent defendants simply do not have the money to pay the bail bondsman 10% of their bail, and given the drug war and rising fear about crime, the percentage of defendants granted a release on their own recognizance has shrunk to only about 15%. The intended purpose of bail is to assure that the defendant will show up for court hearings, since otherwise the bail money will be forfeited. However, bail has become a form of punishment especially for low-income defendants because they can't afford even 10% of the amount. As a result, many languish in jail for months before any trial and verdict. When finally released, they may find their job, housing, property, spouse, and/or children already gone. As Albert Samaha documented in a 2012 investigative article in the *San Francisco Weekly*:

❖ It's the filthy secret of the American judicial system: A majority of county jail inmates have not been convicted of any crime. They sleep and eat among the proven criminals, and they are treated as such, since they are packed into crowded barracks and transported in chains, because they did not have enough money to bail their way out. More than 60% of America's jail population has not been convicted, more than 70% in California.

❖ These inmates held in jail because they cannot afford bail are casualties of a bail system in which freedom is determined not just by a person's perceived risk to society but also by their wealth.

❖ Many people unfairly held in jail because they can't afford to even pay a bail bondsman should be released if they are being held on a less serious crime and don't pose a threat to society. Otherwise, people who live paycheck to paycheck will lose their paycheck and all that comes with it, because they are confined to jail while awaiting trial or other adjudication of their case. Some will lose their homes. Others will lose custody of their children. Many will see their family struggle to make ends meet. Banished to correctional limbo, they will see the world proceeding outside their cells, as their lives remain locked down and frozen.[125]

This outcome due to sentencing guidelines is both unfair to the individuals who are held in jail, though they pose little or no risk of further offenses, and an unnecessary exorbitant cost to the corrections system, and therefore to the tax payer. After all, each jailed convict costs the county over $26,000 a year to be housed[126], while his or her life implodes outside the jail, and any income from a job on hold or terminated is lost to the community and taxpayers, too.

How did this unfairness come about? The Bail Reform Act of 1966 provided that defendants in non-capital crime cases have a right to be released on their own recognizance

---

[125]Albert Samaha, "Barred from Freedom: How Pretrial Detention Ruins Lives", *San Francisco Weekly*, November 21, 2012.
http://www.sfweekly.com/sanfrancisco/barred-from-freedom-how-pretrial-detention-ruins-lives/Content?oid=2187112

[126] A 2014 survey of 17 jail systems in 10 states reporting their costs found the average cost per year per jailed person was $26,098, varying from county to county even within states from a low of $17,382 (Cherokee Cty, GA) to a high of $79,555 (Onondaga Cty, NY-which includes Syracuse); The Price of Jails: Measuring the Taxpayer Cost of Local Incarceration; Vera Institute of Justice, May 2015.

(OR) rather than bail. But in practice, defendants are generally not given this OR release.

A frequent rationale for not offering an OR release is the fear that the defendant won't appear or may even flee the jurisdiction or the country if granted such a release. Yet these fears are flawed. As necessary, a judge can impose additional conditions to make sure the person will appear in court. Accordingly, in determining bail, a judge under the 1966 Bail Reform Act is supposed to require the least restrictive conditions possible, such as ordering a home detention, travel limitations, or a monetary bond. A pretrial incarceration is supposed to be the last resort.

However, due to rising crime rates, policies changed. Law enforcement officials argued that judges should consider the "potential danger a defendant poses to society," and a number of states made public safety another consideration in setting bail. In response, Congress passed the Bail Reform Act of 1984, marking a shift from a concern with poverty and civil liberty in setting bail to assuaging the public's fear of crime and danger.[127]

So how can we fix this problem of unnecessary and expensive bail which low-income arrestees can't afford?

We should return to the original 1966 purpose of setting bail, which was to use the least restrictive approach possible to ensure a person shows up in court. In assessing a case, judges should look at an individual's previous criminal record, if any, as well as to the strength of the case against a person. If the case hinges on a single accuser who knows the accused, that could be a red flag that the accuser might be acting out of revenge.

---

[127]John Goldkamp "Danger and Detention: A Second Generation of Bail Reform," *Journal of Criminal Law and Criminology*, 76(1), 1985, pp. 1-74.

The judge should also consider if the person is employed, or has a partner or family in the area that might be negatively affected by the defendant being locked up. Another consideration favoring no or low bail might be if the person owns a home or has a long-term lease on an apartment in the area. The judge might also issue a stay-away order to keep the defendant from having any contact with the accuser. Still another possibility is for the judge to set the bail low enough for the defendant to meet it by paying the 10% bail money or by arranging for weekly payments.

In short, if a low-income person faces jail because he/she cannot afford bail, the judge should do everything possible to enable the defendant to remain out of jail while the case is proceeding. By doing so, the judge will avoid situations where the defendant's life is ruined due to the time unnecessarily spent in jail awaiting trial or due to being forced into accepting a guilty plea to get out of going to prison for a crime he or she didn't commit.

Prescription # 3: More Legal Assistance for Low-Income Defendants

Legal assistance can really help low-income defendants stay out of prison or get a much reduced sentence. That's because defendants without the financial means to afford an attorney to fight for them may feel they have little choice but to plead guilty and accept a reduced sentence rather than risk — and likely receive — a much longer punishment. Additionally, public defenders or assigned criminal defense lawyers typically suggest that a defendant take a plea, because their high caseload and limited budget limit their ability to take cases to court to fight the charges, regardless of the case's merits. As defense attorney Michelle Alexander explains:

"Most Americans probably have no idea how common it is for people to be convicted without ever having the benefit of legal representation, or how many people plead guilty to crimes they did not commit because of fear of mandatory sentences.

"Approximately 80% of criminal defendants are indigent and thus unable to hire a lawyer. Yet our nation's public defender system is woefully inadequate. The most visible sign of the failed system is the astonishingly large caseloads public defenders routinely carry, making it impossible for them to provide meaningful representation of their clients. Sometimes defenders have well over one hundred clients at a time."[128]

---

[128] Michelle Alexander, *The New Jim Crow: Mass Incarceration in the Age of Colorblindness*, The New Press, 2012.

As Alexander further points out, both types of defense attorneys — public defenders and court-appointed private attorneys — not only are prevented from providing a good defense due to a lack of resources, but they suffer from poor working conditions and low pay, which "discourage good attorneys from participating in the system."[129]

The problem can be resolved by:

➢ More funds should be provided by the county or state or a citizen's initiative to attract more public defenders and court-appointed lawyers, which would allow for reduced caseloads and more time to properly handle a case.

➢ The current *pro bono* system should be expanded with sufficient funds to encourage new lawyers to come to the aid of financially strapped clients. This system, in turn, would provide an outlet for attorneys who are having difficulty finding jobs.

---

[129] Michelle Alexander, *The New Jim Crow: Mass Incarceration in the Age of Colorblindness*, The New Press, 2012.

Prescription # 4: Strict Limits on Immunity of Prosecutors and Judges

While most prosecutors and judges are good citizens devoted to their duties, unfortunately, they operate in a broken criminal justice system in need of serious fixing. A few prosecutors and judges take advantage of the broken system to advance their own agendas, and a few more are given the wrong incentives by the system. For example, they tend to safeguard wealthier constituencies.

Due to increasing economic pressures, justice has become a one-way revolving door through which both judges and prosecutors seek to process cases as quickly as possible. With little incentives to seek the truth, the payoff for many prosecutors is to "win" at all costs in front of judges increasingly inclined to rule in their favor. But in any quest for efficiency rather than justice, society itself begins to suffer.

And as has been shown, civil litigation is increasingly unavailable as a deterrent against or a remedy for prosecutorial misconduct — even when prosecutors engage in criminal conduct. With a handful of exceptions, most prosecutors do not even have written guidelines for differentiating between error and misconduct.

What can be done to ensure prosecutors act in a fair manner? One key strategy is to abolish absolute immunity for prosecutors and introduce a more restricted form of qualified immunity in its place.

Such an approach was suggested in a 2011 *Fordham Law Review* article, in which Margaret Z. Johns made this call for getting rid of absolute prosecutorial immunity:

"The doctrine of absolute prosecutorial immunity in federal civil rights actions is unsupportable. From the point of view of public policy, absolute prosecutorial immunity leads to wrongful prosecutions and convictions, ruins the lives of the wrongly accused, subjects crime victims to the painful and protracted relitigation of their experiences, impairs public safety, wastes public resources, and undermines public respect for, and confidence in, the criminal justice system."[130]

Conservative columnist George Will likewise believes that prosecutorial immunity should be reconsidered.[131] In his view, state and federal legislators should create a fair process called "qualified immunity" that would subject both prosecutors and judges to civil litigation, if they engage in prosecutorial abuse and there is sufficient evidence to hold them to account. Their immunity would be "qualified" when they are shown to have engaged in intentional bad behavior and have not simply made a mistake, which could be excused. Their behavior might be clearly intentional malicious behavior, such as hiding or destroying evidence, particularly evidence the prosecutor knows would be exculpatory. Of course, the line between what is an innocent mistake and what is an intentional heinous act to hide or destroy evidence is subject to interpretation, so it would be up to a judge to determine when a prosecutor has crossed the line.

This qualified immunity for prosecutors would only come into play if they are determined to have abused the process in a criminal case. This requirement would avoid the problem of defendants initiating litigation simply because

---

[130] Margaret Z. Johns, "Unsupportable and Unjustified: A Critique of Absolute Prosecutorial Immunity," *Fordham Law Review*, 80, 2011. http://ir.lawnet.fordham.edu/cgi/viewcontent.cgi?article=4662&context=flr

[131] George Will, "Overcriminalization Plagues U.S. Society," *Tyler Morning Telegraph*, April 9, 2015; http://www.tylerpaper.com/TP-Editorials/217392/overcriminalization-plagues-us-society

they are unhappy with a conviction and sentence against them. The only way a victim of misconduct can currently file a civil action is to defeat any criminal charges against them and prove that "the prosecutor violated clearly established constitutional law with a culpable state of mind." On the other hand, qualified immunity does offer some protections to prosecutors to balance the potential for a defendant's charges against them, in that this immunity offers a complete defense for any prosecutorial actions except for the "most inexcusable misconduct."[132]

In short, qualified immunity would establish a basis for providing victims of intentional prosecutorial misconduct with a remedy against that misconduct, while avoiding a malicious attack on prosecutors by unhappy but justly convicted defendants. Likewise, the same kind of qualified immunity standard should be applied to judges who willfully act unfairly or with bias in a case. Since few judges are ever disciplined by judicial oversight panels, the judges engaging in misconduct should be subject to the potential for civil litigation, if their behavior is shown to be sufficiently egregious.

---

[132]Margaret Z. Johns, "Reconsidering Absolute Prosecutorial Immunity," *Brigham Young University Law Review*, March 1, 2005.

Prescription # 5: Separate Courts for Urban, Suburban and Rural Areas

Separate courts in urban, suburban, and rural areas would also bring more justice to the criminal justice system because of the differences in conditions and perspectives in these different areas. Residents in each area also are unaware of these differences. Most suburban voters in middle and upper income neighborhoods have little idea of ongoing abuses in the criminal justice system. Rural voters are similarly unaware of the abuses, since they are less likely to be affected by high crime rates. Thus, for suburban and rural constituencies alike, the criminal justice system seemingly operates in another universe: one comprising the inner cities.

William J. Stuntz, an evangelical Christian and avowed conservative at Harvard Law School, claimed in *The Collapse of American Criminal Justice* that, "the American system of criminal justice has unraveled before our eyes — a phenomenon that has escaped the notice of most citizens."[133] In Stuntz's view, this lack of awareness among the general population occurred because the middle and upper classes live separate and apart from the urban poor, who are the primary targets of the criminal justice system's machinery.[133]

When those in the middle and upper classes think about how the criminal justice system works, they draw on a misleading picture presented by TV and the movies, which glamorize the police, investigators, and prosecutors. These law enforcement professionals score a win when they solve the crime and toss the criminal in jail, and virtually all criminals depicted on these shows are guilty, so the system

---

[133] Eric Pilch, "Criminal Injustice," *Counterpoint: A Magazine of Politics and Culture*, April 19, 2012.
http://www.counterpointmagazine.org/2012/04/19/criminal-injustice

itself is never at fault. These dramas, suspense thrillers, and action/adventure shows typically try to avoid the stereotypes that fuel racial discrimination by featuring criminals from different social classes -- and often white middle and upper class criminals have starring roles. By contrast, such discrimination is rampant in the real day-to-day criminal justice system. The stories are unrealistic in that they do not depict the real long and drawn-out process and bureaucratic nightmare that confronts a primarily poor, inner city defendant, since crimes are typically solved in a single 30 to 60 minute episode. As Alexander points out:

"Those who have been swept within the criminal justice system know that the way the system actually works bears little resemblance to what happens on television or in movies. Full-blown trials of guilt or innocence rarely occur; many people never even meet with an attorney; witnesses are routinely paid and coerced by the government; police regularly stop and search people for no reason whatsoever; penalties for many crimes are so severe that innocent people plead guilty, accepting plea bargains to avoid harsh mandatory sentences; and children, even as young as fourteen, are sent to adult prisons."[134]

What can be done so that prisons and their inmates are no longer out of sight and out of mind? The following prescription might provide one way to increase awareness to assure a fairer result, as well as reduce the costs of unnecessary imprisonment.

> To allow for the differences in culture and customs of the urban, suburban, and rural areas, separate courts

---

[134] Michelle Alexander, *The New Jim Crow: Mass Incarceration in the Age of Colorblindness,* The New Press, 2012.

should be set up for urban, suburban, and rural areas in order to prosecute individuals closer to their own community of residence.[135]

➤ These separate jurisdictions might also have separate slates of prosecutors and judges, so citizens vote only for the prosecutors and judges for their area.

➤ The use of separate courts in different jurisdictions might contribute to both reductions in sentences and less incarceration. For example, judges in a local area might be more receptive to consider alternative sentences like halfway houses or probation rather than incarcerations.

---

[135] Separate voting in these jurisdictions was previously proposed in Chapter 5 of this book.

Prescription # 6: Reduce the High Rate of Incarceration

Anything to reduce the high rate of incarceration will also contribute to reducing costs in the system. The number of inmates is so huge that in the United States today there are more prisoners than farmers. While most prisoners in America are from urban communities, most prisons are now in rural areas... prisons have become a 'growth industry' in rural America.[136]

This sheer size of the prison-industrial system requires that it support a vast number of employees — about 800,000 individuals nationally. Moreover, in 2010, the annual cost to keep someone imprisoned, such as in a Federal Bureau of Prisons facility, was $28,284.16, whereas the annual cost of probation supervision was only $3,938.35, making that a much less expensive option for punishment where feasible.[137]

Yet despite the visions of incoming rural prosperity due to the rural prison boom, prisons are not a great boon either to the rural or inner city economies.

A reason that a local prison is not the economic benefit it is cracked up to be is the following:

❖ First, urban centers lose out because the rural prison boom pulls a substantial number of dollars from urban to rural America. That's because "prison inmates are counted in the populations of the towns and counties in which they are incarcerated and not in their home neighborhoods." As a result, the biggest loser is the

---

[136]Tracy Huling, "Building a Prison Economy in Rural America," from *Invisible Punishment*, Marc Mauer and Meda Chesney-Lind, Editors. The New Press. 2002, http://www.prisonpolicy.org/scans/building.html

[137] "Newly Available: Costs of Incarceration and Supervision in FY 2010," *The Third Branch News*, United States Courts, June 23, 2011, http://tinyurl.com/apyw4qh

urban communities of color, as half of all American prisoners are African-American and one-sixth are Latino. These minorities' already troubled home communities therefore become even more impoverished. The communities also lose political representation and power, as prisoners can no longer vote, and yet they are counted as part of the population where they are serving time.

❖ Secondly, rural communities lose out, too, because the majority of prison jobs do not go to people already living in the community. Rather, they go to others who commute there. Moreover, the mere location of a prison in a town can discourage other kinds of industries from coming to the area.

How can we keep the sheer number of prisons, and the costs of prison maintenance and prisoner upkeep, from sapping the economies of both rural and urban communities? We can reduce such costs through the following:

➤ We can scale back the War on Drugs, which has not significantly reduced the drug supply. Scaling back will save our economy billions. While scaling back on inner city drug sweeps is controversial, it would reduce the number of prisoners incarcerated and the costs to incarcerate them.

➤ We can reduce the length of sentences given to non-violent drug offenders and defendants charged with other non-violent crimes, or we can offer alternative sentences based on the nature of the crime. For example, drug offenders might be sentenced to attend drug-court programs — programs that already have proved very successful. Other options might be sentences that involve community service, participation in job training programs, or internships.

➢ Judges can sentence convicted non-violent defendants to halfway houses, home detention, or community service programs in their home community wherever possible, particularly if the defendants have spouses or children.

➢ The prisons can provide more faith-based programs in the final year of detention to prepare inmates for successful re-entry into society, as previously discussed in Chapter 2. Such programs will help to reduce recidivism -- the further commission of crime.

<u>Prescription # 7: End the War on Marijuana to Reduce
Violence and Possibly Bring Revenue to Cash-Starved States
and Cities</u>

There is no good reason to keep this war going,
because it has proved so costly and hasn't worked to stop the
use of marijuana for either medical or recreational use. Much
as happened with prohibition, it makes more economic sense
to decriminalize marijuana like a traffic ticket or to simply
regulate and tax it, rather than spend millions on an
ineffective program. A look at the cost figures shows this.

As of December 6, 2012, the U.S. Federal and State
Government spent over $38 billion in the 2012 War on
Drugs.[138] Yet the war on drugs has been an utter failure,
according to the Associated Press:

"After 40 years, the United States' war on
drugs has cost $1 trillion and hundreds of thousands
of lives, and for what? Drug use is rampant and
violence even more brutal and widespread...In the
grand scheme, it has not been successful."[139]

Although citizens associate the drug trade with crime
and violence, the drugs themselves are not the cause of these
activities; rather, the crime and violence occur mostly because
drugs are illegal. The bottom line is, "we [America'] would
have a lot less violence without a war on drugs." According
to economist Art Carden:

"The war on drugs has been a dismal failure.
It's high time to end prohibition. Even if you aren't

---

[138] "The Drug War Clock, December 6, 2012, citing the Office of National Drug
Control Policy, and Jeffrey A. Miron & Kathrine Waldock, "The Budgetary
Impact of Drug Prohibition," 2010.
[139] "AP IMPACT: After 40 years, $1 trillion, US War on Drugs has failed to
meet any of its goals." Fox News.com, May 13, 2010, http://tinyurl.com/apngetu

willing to go whole-hog and legalize all drugs, at the very least we should legalize marijuana."

"Prohibition is a textbook example of a policy with negative unintended consequences... Vigorous enforcement means higher prices and higher revenues for drug dealers."

"The paradox is that the government's efforts to make us safer have put us in greater danger, as America's inner cities have turned into war zones and eroded the very freedoms we hold dear."[140]

Business writers in conservative business publications, such as *Forbes*, have strongly advocated ending the drug wars, and at the very least, decriminalizing marijuana. In fact, 19 states and Washington, D.C. have decriminalized possession of small amounts of marijuana.[141]

Decriminalization would have a significant economic benefit. Out of the drug arrests made back in 2009, more than half (858,408) were for cannabis violations — with about 89% of those arrests for possession only— and we are on pace to reach 780,000 cannabis arrests this year.[142] Fortunately, far fewer are actually incarcerated for cannabis. Estimates range from 10,000-20,000 for those in prison for marijuana possession only.[142,143] At an average of $30,000 per prisoner we spend $300-600 million on cannabis incarcerations for cannabis possession, and untold more for processing the additional three quarters of a million people annually arrested for cannabis possession.

---

[140] Art Carden, "Let's Be Blunt: It's Time to End the Drug War." http://tinyurl.com/a98cpyz

[141] http://krwg.org/post/97-texas-marijuana-convictions-are-possession

[142] "The Drug War Clock," citing Uniform Crime Reports, Federal Bureau of Investigation," http://www.drugsense.org/cms/wodclock

[143]

As of this writing, more than 50% of the U.S. population supports legalizing pot, and a growing number of states and cities have passed laws that make it legal to grow and distribute medical marijuana. One of the latest states to allow the recreational use of marijuana is Alaska, long a conservative bastion in the United States. So if Alaska can opt to legalize the recreational use of pot, why can't other states?

However, Attorney General Sessions has already expressed his determination to oppose and prosecute to the fullest extent possible under the law any form of legal, decriminalized or medical marijuana. This is one issue where conservatives may favor a federal approach, while liberals advocate for state rights.

Business investors have made the case that if marijuana in all forms was legalized, it could be taxed by federal, state, and city governments, and provide significant revenue, particularly for cash-starved states and cities.

How and why should we handle the possibility of legalizing marijuana? Some possible ways include:

➢ Decriminalize the possession of small quantities of recreational marijuana so it is considered only an infraction, such as a citation or speeding ticket, in certain test states and observe the results. If the negative consequences of decriminalization are small, more states will decriminalize it.

➢ Observe closely what happens in those states that have legalized medical marijuana, and then take steps to legalize medical marijuana elsewhere if prudent.

➢ Observe the results obtained in states that have legalized and taxed all marijuana. If the results show minimal adverse consequences, allow more states to legalize recreational marijuana and invest the money that is now going toward interdiction and prison building back to government coffers, along with the income from state marijuana taxes. If marijuana is legalized, it should be done in a responsible manner. Washington State's policy seems a sound one to adopt, since it includes these provisions:

1. Provide "accountable oversight by an agency of government:" A state agency should write regulations regarding the growing, producing, and selling of marijuana. These regulations should include tight limitations on advertising and the prevention of access to pot by minors. The agency should have the authority to issue licenses to growers, producers, and sellers and to enforce adherence to the rules.
2. Include a well-funded marijuana education program based on science rather than ideology.
3. Have a well-funded prevention program to help young people use marijuana wisely and avoid abusing it.
4. Establish a treatment program for marijuana dependence.
5. Require an evaluation of the new model's impact.
6. Make state funds available for research on marijuana by the state's two major research universities.[144]

---

[144] "The End of the War on Marijuana," November 9, 2012.
http://www.cnn.com/2012/11/08/opinion/roffman-pot-legalization/index.html

Prescription # 8: Establish More Drug Treatment and More Drug Courts

As noted in Prescriptions #6 and #7, the cost of fighting drugs over the last 40 years has been in the trillions. We are on track to spend 40 billion dollars in the war on drugs this year alone.[145] Even though the U.S. has devoted many resources to drug interdiction, this prohibition approach has not worked. More than 22 million Americans use illegal drugs as of this writing, and for most addicts, predatory crime — larceny, shoplifting, sneak thievery, burglary, embezzlement, robbery, and so forth — is a necessary way of life in order to support oneself. Drug addiction makes it difficult to maintain a job, and addicts often turn to crime to get the monies for food, shelter, and to obtain the drugs they "need," lest they suffer debilitating withdrawal symptoms.[146]

Aside from addictions to cocaine, amphetamines, and other controlled drugs, opiate addiction, once restricted to urban minority communities, has reached epidemic proportions throughout the heartland. It was even a bipartisan issue in the 2016 presidential campaign. Physicians overprescribing pain medications for illnesses and injuries may have been responsible for turning once responsible, respectable patients to addiction. Then, once hooked, they become slaves to their craving. In part because of this genesis of addiction, physicians and scientists commonly agree that addiction is better viewed as an illness than as a moral failing.

---

[145] http://www.drugsense.org/cms/wodclock

[146] "Drug Addiction, Crime or Disease?" Interim and Final Reports of the Joint Committee of the American Bar Association and the American Medical Association on Narcotic Drugs, 1961, http://www.druglibrary.org/schaffer/library/studies/dacd/appendixa_9.htm

Unfortunately, once in the grips of an addiction, individuals can remain stuck, since very few of those affected can afford the kind of treatment center that cured Rush Limbaugh or other high-profile celebrities. Even many middle and upper income addicts don't have the kinds of funds to join these expensive "kick-the-addiction" programs. So this is a widespread problem that affects all classes in society; it is no longer confined to the inner cities, and it's time to shed its gangster image, because addiction affects us all.

Thus, it's time to change our approach to those who use illegal drugs by offering drug treatment plans rather than punishment. From a cost-savings standpoint, drug treatment reduces expenditures. These big financial savings to society result from less "violent and property crimes, prison expenses, court and criminal costs, emergency room visits, child abuse and neglect, lost child support, foster care and welfare costs, reduced productivity, unemployment, and victimization."[147]

Moreover, according to the National Institute of Drug Abuse (NIDA), drug treatment can "cut drug abuse in half, reduce criminal activity up to 80%, and reduce arrests up to 64%."[148] From a healthcare perspective, the spread of HIV/AIDS, hepatitis, and other infectious diseases is decreased, as such diseases are often passed on by drug addicts sharing needles.

---

[147] "Drug Addiction, Crime or Disease?" Interim and Final Reports of the Joint Committee of the American Bar Association and the American Medical Association on Narcotic Drugs, 1961, http://www.druglibrary.org/schaffer/library/studies/dacd/appendixa_9.htm

[148] "NIDA Announces Recommendations to Treat Drug Abusers, Save Money and Reduce Crime," *NIH News*, July 24, 2006; http://www.nih.gov/news/pr/jul2006/nida-24.htm

Extensive research has shown that treatment for abusers in the criminal justice system as well as for those living outside it has proven effective. As the National Institute of Drug Abuse (NIDA) notes: "Treatment is an effective intervention for drug abusers... Longitudinal outcome studies find that those who participate in community-based drug abuse treatment programs commit fewer crimes than those who do not."[149]

Accordingly, we should establish a new drug treatment approach for those in the criminal justice system. Here's how we can successfully implement it:

➢ Encourage sentencing changes to allow some nonviolent drug offenders out of prison early, if they complete an intensive treatment program.

➢ Instead of sentencing non-violent drug offenders to prison, judges should find less restrictive penalties, such as time served, coupled with treatment and probation or community service.

➢ Incorporate drug abuse treatment programs into a variety of criminal justice setting. These might include treatment as a condition of probation, drug courts that combine judicial monitoring and sanctions with treatment, in-prison and then community-based treatment after the individual is discharged, and treatment while the ex-convict is being supervised under parole or probation.[150]

---

[149] "Principles of Drug Abuse Treatment for Criminal Justice Populations – A Research-Based Guide," National Institute of Drug Abuse, National Institutes of Health, http://tinyurl.com/bc5aco9

[150] "Drug Facts: Treatment for Drug Abusers in the Criminal Justice System," Revised July 2006, http://tinyurl.com/by8kb7p

➤ Mainstream the use of drug courts for nonviolent offenders, an approach that has worked around the country. It has offered addicts an opportunity to participate in a treatment program, along with help in finding work if they are successful in completing the program. The quarter of offenders who graduate from these drug courts have greatly reduced rates of recidivism and re-arrest rates, and these programs cost our cities and states significantly less than standard prison sentences.[151,152,153,154]

➤ Extend cost-effective programs that work to the public at large in less restrictive settings.

➤ As a last resort, consider the Portuguese approach of monitoring drug addicts and providing them with free methadone. Compared to 312 deaths per million from drug-related deaths in the U.S., Portugal has only 6 per million. This doesn't solve the drug problem, but it does reduce its horrific consequences. The cost of such treatment is a tiny fraction of the cost of what we continue to spend on the War on Drugs.[155]

---

[151] "Drug Court Helps Addicts Kick Habit – and Charges," *San Francisco Chronicle,* November 12, 2012, pp. A1, A9, http://www.sfgate.com/crime/article/Drug-court-Addicts-kick-habit-charges-4028550.php
[152] San Francisco Collaborative Courts, *Research Review*, May 2009.
[153] State of New Jersey, Office of the Public Defender, http://www.state.nj.us/defender/drugcrt.shtml
[154] John Rodor, Wendy Townsend, and Avinash Sing Bhati: "Recidivism Rates for Drug Court Graduates: Nationally Based Estimates, Final Report," July, 2003. https://www.ncjrs.gov/pdffiles1/201229.pdf
[155] Nicholas Kristof, "How to Win a War on Drugs. Unlike the United States, Portugal treats addiction as a medical problem, not a criminal justice issue," *New York Times*, Sept. 24, 2017.

Prescription # 9: Overhaul the Criminal Justice System

A complete overhaul of the criminal justice system is needed, as reflected in a bill to do just this, which was introduced in 2009 by former Senator Jim Webb. Among the many reasons for doing this are these huge figures, which show how expensive and ineffective our criminal justice system really is:

❖ With 5% of the world's population, our country now houses 25% of the world's reported prisoners.

❖ The number of incarcerated drug offenders has soared 1,200% since 1980.

❖ Four times as many mentally ill people are in prisons as in mental health hospitals.

❖ Approximately 1 million gang members reside in the U.S., many of them foreign-based, and Mexican cartels operate in more than 230 communities across the country.

❖ Post-incarceration re-entry programs are haphazard and often nonexistent, making it extremely difficult for ex-offenders to become full, contributing members of society.

Such statistics are what led Senator Webb to author his National Criminal Justice Commission Act (S. 306), Senator Webb to effect the following reforms. He sought to:

"Create a blue-ribbon commission to look at every aspect of our criminal justice system with an eye toward reshaping the criminal justice system from top to bottom ...[It is] designed to prevent, deter, and reduce crime and violence, improve cost-effectiveness, and ensure the interests of justice.....It is time to bring together the best minds in America to analyze the criminal justice system in its entirety, to examine its interlocking parts, to learn what works and what does not, and make recommendations for reform."[156]

Webb's proposed bill was designed to create the first comprehensive national review of crime policy in 45 years. He worked tirelessly to enact the bill for three years, and lined up more than 100 key supporters in law enforcement, politics, and other fields.

Initially, his bill looked like it would do well, after he received approval of the Senate Judiciary Committee on Jan. 21, 2010, and the House of Representatives passed it on July 28, 2010.

Unfortunately, the bill ran into rough waters, as it was blocked in the Senate later that year. When Webb introduced it again in February 2011, he gained support for his proposed National Criminal Justice Commission from more than 100 organizations from every political and philosophical perspective. However, the bill fell a mere three votes short of obtaining a supermajority (sixty votes) required for passage.[157]

---

[156] http://www.humanejustice.org/background_criminal_justice.htm
[157] http://sentencing.typepad.com/sentencing_law_and_policy/2011/10/senate-republicans-block-jim-webbs-bill-for-creating-national-criminal-justice-commission.html

Webb's bill became a victim of partisan gridlock. What should be done now? How can we do it better? There appears to be an opening.

Liberals may have gotten the "jump" on conservatives on this issue, but conservatives are finally catching up. Supreme Court Justice Anthony Kennedy, an appointee of Ronald Reagan, testified before a Financial Services and General Government Subcommittee, where he stated that "this idea of total incarceration just isn't working." Further, he stated that "California, my home state, had 187,000 people in jail, at a cost of over $30,000 a prisoner, compared to the amount they gave to schoolchildren; that's about $3,500 a year."[158]

Businessman Charles Koch, oft pilloried by liberals, has supported this pressing need for criminal justice reform, too. As he has concluded:

> "Reversing over-criminalization and mass incarceration will improve societal well-being in many respects, most notably by decreasing poverty. Today, approximately 50 million people (about 14 percent of the population) are at or below the U.S. poverty rate. Fixing our criminal system could reduce the overall poverty rate as much as 30%, dramatically improving the quality of life throughout society — especially for the disadvantaged."[159]

---

[158] Jess Bravin, "Two Supreme Court Justices Say Criminal-Justice System Isn't Working," *The Wall Street Journal*, March 24, 2015.

[159] Charles G. Koch and Mark V. Holden, "The Overcriminalization of America. How to reduce poverty and improve race relations by rethinking our justice system." *Politico Magazine*, January 7, 2015. http://www.politico.com/magazine/story/2015/01/overcriminalization-of-america-113991.html#.VXXcU03bKUk

Most tellingly, the conservative Heritage Foundation identifies a number of examples of overcriminalization and concludes:

❖ "Criminal justice reform is about more than policy debates in Congress or legal procedure; it is about how the lives and fortunes of ordinary Americans are threatened by abuse of the law. The criminal justice reform movement should focus on telling the stories of those who are affected by an overly zealous government and the excessive power of the state.

❖ Only by identifying the problem and highlighting why it matters will any meaningful change take place. Over-criminalization is not an easy problem to solve, but it is one that demands our attention."[160]

Once the problems have been identified, Webb's National Justice Commission Act or a bipartisan or Republican-led version of it is precisely what is now needed. While Webb's original act did not gain enough support for passage and Senator Webb has retired, in the future, it is critical that other legislators pick up the torch for a comprehensive overhaul of our criminal justice system. Perhaps recent across-the-aisle alliances, such as those involving Senators Mike Lee (R), Dick Durbin (D), Ted Cruz (R), Patrick Leahy (D), Cory Booker (D) and Rand Paul (R)[161,162] could put such a plan forward. Support from other

---

[160] Jordan Richardson, "Shining a Light on Overcriminalization", The Heritage Foundation, June 1, 2015;
http://www.heritage.org/research/reports/2015/06/shining-a-light-on-overcriminalization
[161]http://www.lee.senate.gov/public/index.cfm/2015/2/lee-durbin-introduce-smarter-sentencing-act-of-2015

conservative Senators and conservative Congressmen in the House should also be encouraged.

However, reducing mass incarceration cannot just be a federal effort. States have to be involved, too, since "90% of those incarcerated are in state or local facilities....mass incarceration needs to be dismantled one state at a time."[163]

Thus, clearly there is a major role here for states' rights. States whose legislatures are reliably conservative or reliably liberal can most easily effect change in policy without jeopardizing their political future.

> Legislatures in those states should take up the mantle of criminal justice reform. They should reduce the bloated prison population by revising sentencing guidelines to reduce sentences or permit greater judicial discretion in sentencing. They should also provide further support for programs designed to train inmates for successful re-entry into society.

> Other states should make attempts at bipartisan criminal justice reform.

Such efforts to accomplish significant criminal justice reform are essential to implement now while it is still possible to create change politically. Otherwise, the danger is that liberal activists may convince defendants to take truly radical action to crash the system.[164] For example, Michelle Alexander has urged defendants to opt to go to trial rather

---

[162] http://www.paul.senate.gov/?p=press_release&id=1192
[163] Marc Mauer and David Cole, "How to Lock Up Fewer People," *New York Times*, May 24, 2015.
[164] Michelle Alexander, "Go to Trial: Crash the Justice System," *The New York Times*, Sunday Review, The Opinion Pages, March 10, 2012; http://tinyurl.com/avo9rjb

than taking pleas, and if enough defendants choose this option, then the courts will be overwhelmed and the criminal justice system will literally grind to a halt. Meanwhile, many dangerous defendants may be released on bail, putting many communities at risk of an increase in property crimes and crimes of violence. At the same time, without such reform, a growing number of radical activist groups, such as the anarchist antifascist Antifa collectives,[165] are poised to stir up violent confrontations, overwhelming the police, who are unable to either stop the violence or arrest the miscreants. These are the "pretty bad dudes on the other side also," that President Trump referred to while condemning white supremacists. He was right to criticize both despite continuing liberal objections to his failure to decry only white supremacists for the Charlottesville violence. Such violent encounters are growing, reflected in the upheavals in Berkeley and San Francisco, where some counter-protesters assembled to still conservative voices.

Thus, efforts to reform the system by conservatives are more necessary than ever, before liberal and radical voices take control of any reform effort and act to increase violence that endangers us all.

---

[165] Edmon de Haro, "The Rise of the Violent Left," *The Atlantic*, September 2017.

ABOUT THE AUTHOR

Paul Brakke is a scientist based in central Arkansas. He became interested in studying the criminal justice system when his life was turned upside down after his wife was falsely accused of aggravated assault for allegedly trying to run over a 12 year old boy with her car. This happened because a group of kids and some neighbors wanted her out of the neighborhood. Eventually, the Brakkes were forced to move as part of a plea agreement, since otherwise, Brakke's wife faced a possible 16 year jail sentence if the case went to trial and she lost. He has previously told his wife's story in *American Justice?*, along with a preliminary critique of the criminal justice system. That book's website is at www.americanjusticethebook.com. Paul Brakke has also written several other books:

The Price of Justice in America
Cops Aren't Such Bad Guys
The Great National Divides

CONTACT US

For more information:

AMERICAN LEADERSHIP BOOKS
Little Rock, Arkansas
(501) 503-8614
brakkep@gmail.com